DESIGNERS' HANDBOOK OF BOOKLETS AND BROCHURES

Manufactured in
Singapore.

Designers' Handbook of
Booklets & Brochures
Library of Congress
Catalog Card Number
94-067218
ISBN 1-883915-03-1

RC Publications
**President and
Publisher:**
Howard Cadel
**Vice President and
Editor:**
Martin Fox
Creative Director:
Andrew Kner
**Managing Director,
Book Projects:**
Linda Silver
Assistant Art Director:
Michele L. Trombley
**Administrative
Assistant:**
Nancy Silver

Winning Designs from
Print *Magazine's*
National Design Competition

DESIGNERS'

HAND-BOOK

of Booklets

&

Brochures

Managing Director
Linda Silver

Writer/Editor
Pamela A. Ivinski

Art Director
Andrew Kner

Assistant Art Director
Michele L. Trombley

Published by
RC Publications, Inc.
New York, NY

CONTENTS

7 Corporate Communications

39 RETAIL SALES

Educational and Cultural Institutions

65

50

123

143

159

Welcome to the first volume of *PRINT*'s newest book series: the *Designers' Handbook of Booklets & Brochures*. As in previous *PRINT* books, we feature the best of the works shown in our Regional Design Annual, reproduced here in generously-sized visuals. Newly added is useful information for the designer: Each piece is accompanied by a short essay reporting on client specifications, sources for imagery, page sizes, types of stock and ink, and so forth. In addition, the featured booklets and brochures have been organized by categories and sub-categories, for the reader's ease in comparing examples within specific genres, and each category and sub-category is introduced with commentary detailing design strategies and trends within that group.

The booklets and brochures in this *Designers' Handbook* have been divided into seven general categories, related to the type of booklet or brochure and the nature of the client: Corporate Communications, Retail Sales, Educational and Cultural Institutions, Annual Reports, Design and Printing, Paper Companies, and Tourism and Travel. Within each of these categories, the pieces are divided again into more specific groups, such as annual reports for health industries, non-profit institutions, insurance companies, etc.

Each individual piece is accompanied by a short essay describing the work's creation, answering questions such as: Who was the intended audience for the piece? Where did the original idea come from? How much freedom was the designer allowed in developing the concept? What were the client's restrictions? What kinds of paper stock and ink were used, and why? How was the imagery selected? How do the various parts of the piece interrelate? Why was the format chosen? What kinds of software were used? The featured designers give us a glimpse of the creative process; and not just the triumphs, but the successful compromises, too: French-fold pages used because a heavy stock was unavailable, the revamping of previously-used imagery to save money.

PRINT's *Designers' Handbook of Booklets & Brochures* intends to meet the ever more complex needs of designers with this wealth of information, now arranged by category for ease of use. As a reference tool, the book provides visual ideas, conceptual examples, technical information, and even moral support—yes, it's possible to create a terrific design despite the most restrictive conditions. We hope that you'll spend many hours perusing its pages, and that your design will benefit as a result.
—*Pamela A. Ivinski*

Corporate Communications

The corporate communications materials presented in this section can be divided into four types: capability and image brochures; recruitment literature; reports intended for external audiences such as customers, clients, and investors; and reports for internal distribution. Judging from the examples shown here, designers and their clients agree that brightly colored illustration is the most effective way to convey a message in this type of communication, though illustration can mean anything from the most simplified, blocky, children's book–type image to highly abstract, manipulated photo compositions. But in an "interactive" age, some designers are anxious to go beyond straight print and incorporate gimmicks like half sheets and short pages into their brochures; even drink stirrers and foreign currency are glued into booklets.

As might be expected, communications geared toward "human resources," such as recruiting literature and the brochure for a headhunting firm, stick with warm colors and bold, friendly, fine-art illustration. The same type of imagery is found, too, in brochures for companies offering difficult-to-explain technologically-oriented services, as in AXIS's piece for Software AG, a supplier of "information solutions," with its angular, cartoon-like businessman figure by Terry Allen. Brochures for other companies in related industries, like the Decisionmark "Decide" piece by Pattee Design, forgo a hand-drawn look in favor of stylized photo collages by Pierre-Yves Goavec. A spiral-bound book for Eastman Kodak's Professional and Printing Imagery division, created by Buck & Pulleyn, exploits the advertised "color management" services to the maximum extent by printing Wayne Calabrese's amusing photographs (monkey toys, the bride and groom from a wedding cake) in the most surreal, saturated colors imaginable.

Like the Kodak piece, the capability brochures for design businesses shown here strive the hardest for bigger and better. A large slipcased, spiral-bound book for SHR Perceptual Services utilizes glossy gatefold photos (opening out to spreads measuring 16 1/2" x 14") to evoke high-quality corporate design. Even bigger is Michael Mabry Design's 11" x 17" spiral-bound booklet for Deepa Textiles, designers of office furniture fabric. Philippe Weisbecker's charming handdrawn collages, printed on a flecked beige uncoated stock, accompanied by uncrowded text lines, evoke the special care taken by a company that says, "you can order from the menu. Or you can come into to the kitchen and tell us what you're in the mood for."

At the other extreme, a number of small pieces shown here turn cost-conscious simplicity into an advantage. Donna Mehalke's fluid, fashion illustration–type wash drawings, in a tiny (7" x 7"), slipcased brochure, capture both the comfort and stylishness of Larry Stuart "Essentials" shoes. Yet, small needn't mean simple. To reposition Lee Apparel for younger consumers, Willoughby Design's mainly photographic image book is enlivened with inserts like postcards, paper dolls, and a pull-out poster. And Sayles Graphic Design's book for Cutler Travel Marketing can be filled with customized inserts relating to specific destinations, like matchbooks and drink stirrers from resort hotels.

Because many of these capability and image brochures advertise abstract services, designers are relatively free to lean toward conceptual imagery, within the limits of corporate "protocol." For example, Peterson & Company's brochure for Data Race (pp. 20–21), a company that deals in "multiplexing systems," features brightly colored, people-friendly illustrations, rather than complex technical information, to attract new, non-tech customers. A brochure for the geodemographic software firm, Decisionmark, by Pattee Design (this spread), similarly employs stylized photographic collages to represent the "creative" as well as "analytical" side of decision making. Materials by Copeland Hirthler Design+ Communications for Equifax financial services, on the other hand, use more straightforward photo collages for an elegant effect that will appeal to the executive crowd (pp. 16–17). Ison Design, in a spiral-bound brochure for Connor Formed Metal Parts (p. 27), combines abstract photo imagery with duotone employee portraits, product shots, gatefold charts and graphs, and short-page diagrams to reposition the employee-owned company as far more than a "bid-by-job" supplier.

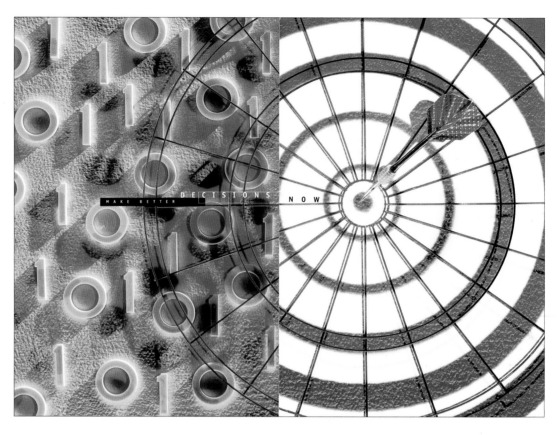

Design Firm:
Pattee Design, Inc.,
Des Moines, Iowa
Art Director:
Steve Pattee
Designers:
Kelly Stiles, Steve Pattee
Photographer:
Pierre-Yves Goavec
Copywriter:
Mike Condon
Printer:
Holm Graphics

Decisionmark sells data—geodemographic software—to decision-makers. In order to reach a Fortune 1000 audience, Pattee Design shaped this "Decide" booklet to emphasize the creative as well as analytical side of the decision-making process, rather than merely expounding the attributes of the company's software. Objects including computer-related paraphernalia are arranged against a highly-textured paper to form images such as a digital-code dartboard or a smiley-face with icon eyes. These visuals represent the creative function as a compromise between technology and humanity. Commissioned from San Francisco photographer Pierre-Yves Goavec, the brightly-colored spreads alternate with "analytical" black-and-white text spreads that provide information on the company and its product. While Decisionmark wanted a perfect-bound book, the message content, at only 22 pages, was too small. Pattee incorporated a french fold in Potlatch Eloquence Silk to add heft to the 7 3/4" x 11 5/8" book.

DECISIONMARK CORP.

Sometimes a

FRESH perspective is all that's **NECESSARY**

"People think visually. Our tools translate lists, attributes, questions and answers into pictures our customers can see."

Now you can play "what if" with your marketplace as easily as you balance your checkbook. There are no tricky algorithms to master, no long strings of programming code to decipher. Just you. Your mouse. A plain English table of contents. And a world of business opportunity.

Decisionmark products and services enable you to create your own unique, evolving database – information you can transform (in seconds) into a virtual world of meaningful, easy-to-see, often unexpected relationships. At last, you can think in concert with your data. Zoom in, zoom out. Point. Click. Turn tables and charts into streets, addresses, houses, customers!

Build new bridges that you and your people can cross together with your eyes wide open and your objectives clearly in sight.

■ Decisionmark base products connect you with the data you need to realize the promise of geodemographic marketing – including maps of the U.S., states, counties, DMAs, MSAs and streets, as well as five-digit zip code and census block group boundaries. Also included are more than 500 population, housing, economic and agricultural census attributes for every state, county, zip code or census block group. Current and five-year projections are provided for many of these attributes.

■ Select the geography for your project, then a menu of attributes appears. Use your mouse to simply check off the criteria you're looking for, and in seconds, you'll have a virtual view of your market. For the first time, you'll be able to really see where your business comes from (or could come from). Demographic and lifestyle data synergistically weave with your information to speed comprehension and improve decision-making.

■ Through relationships with leading list, demographic, lifestyle and specialty database providers, Decisionmark enables you to access a world of information with a single call. All data is shipped map-, graph- and table-ready. The installation program included with each order saves time and makes it easy to load your new data and use it yourself, without outside assistance.

Blaze new trails

"We have a Windows program with no File menu — a certain death wish in the opinion of many software developers. It's non-standard. We believe, however, it's better and our customers will see this."

THE **power** HANDS

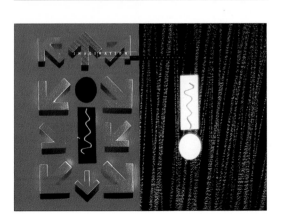

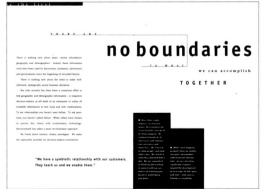

THERE ARE **no boundaries** TO WHAT we can accomplish TOGETHER

"We have a symbiotic relationship with our customers. They teach us and we enable them."

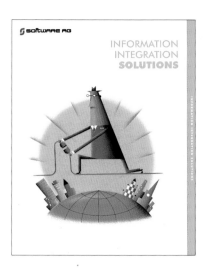

Design Firm:
AXIS Communications,
Washington, DC
Art Director/Designer:
Craig Byers
Illustrator:
Terry Allen

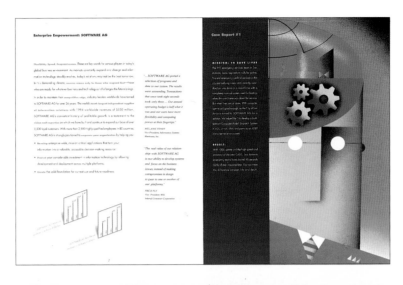

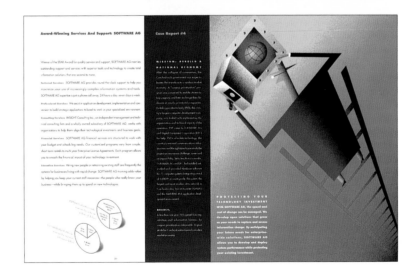

Software AG is the world's tenth-largest independent supplier of information solutions. AXIS Communications created a collateral system for the company, from which these primary marketing pieces were derived. The main "Solving" brochure (measuring 8 1/2" x 11") displays the new palette developed by AXIS to distinguish product families. Conceptual illustrations by Terry Allen combine in spreads with text pages giving company statistics and product information (printed in blue and orange as well as black ink) on a smooth Warren Vintage Velvet stock. Inset between the pages of these spreads are short pages, printed in white on a slightly rougher Beckett Expression in black. The short pages feature case reports, like the Computer-Aided Dispatch System developed by Software AG for the San Antonio, Texas, 911 emergency services. Complementary three-fold brochures employ Allen's illustrations on the covers, with full-page, full-color photographs of company employees within. The design of this marketing system also had to be flexible enough to permit for its reprinting—in German.

MG Design Associates offers a range of services centered around the creation of exhibits for trade shows. Tanagram was hired to produce this brochure in conjunction with a self-promotional exhibit for MG Design, and the design of the exhibit was based on the line-art used on the brochure's cover. By constructing images that communicated like an MG Design exhibit—bold and direct, but layered with information—Tanagram continued the exhibit/brochure synergy. Because the immediate impact of the images was most important, the designers strove for a billboard effect, with each spread opening to 21 $1/2$" x 8 $1/2$", and text kept to a minimum. The brochure's color images were generated in Adobe Photoshop by Tanagram's designers, except for exhibit shots, which were taken from MG's archives and stylized by Tanagram. The images were separated to C, M, and K plates, but on press, MG Design's corporate colors were used: dark purple, olive green, and mustard yellow.

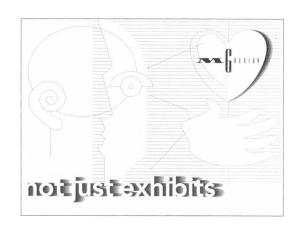

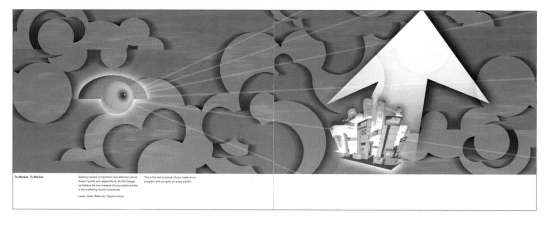

Design Firm:
Tanagram, Inc.,
Chicago, Illinois
Art Director:
Eric Wagner
Designers:
Eric Wagner, David
Kaplan, Erik DeBat
Illustrators:
Eric Wagner, David
Kaplan, Erik DeBat,
Anthony Ma, Grant Davis

Design Firm:
Buck & Pulleyn,
Rochester, New York
Art Director:
Kathy Cairo
Photographer:
Wayne Calabrese
Copywriter:
George Haefner
Printer:
Monroe Litho, Inc.

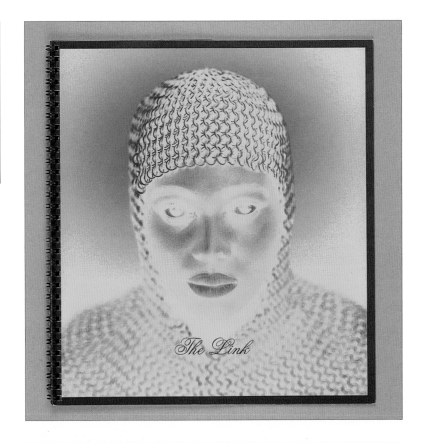

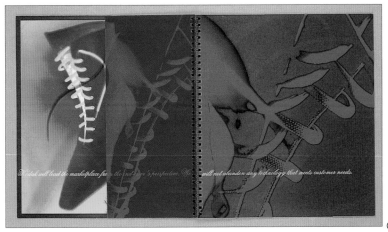

Eastman Kodak's Professional and Printing Imagery division wanted to make a major statement defining and embodying its "color management" capabilities at 1995's DRUPA, an enormous international trade show. Buck & Pulleyn, hired to produce a give-away brochure, saw the problem of its design as "cooking for chefs": creating something that would impress a visually sophisticated audience. Photographs were commissioned from Wayne Calabrese of CR$_2$ Studios, and printed—in glowing hues—on a 6-color press using 4-color process, six flat colors, and two varnishes. To underscore the brochure's goal of presenting Kodak color management as the master link that connects all the components in the color imaging chain, playful images—a woman in a chain-mail headdress, plastic monkey toys linked arm-in-arm, the bride and groom on a wedding cake—are used to illustrate the theme. Text is printed on half-sheets inserted between the spreads, which are visually linked to the full sheets by the use of a varnish spelling out "link" on one side, and a differently-colored version of the spread's visual motif on the other. The brochure measures 9 1/2" x 10 3/4".

EASTMAN KODAK COMPANY

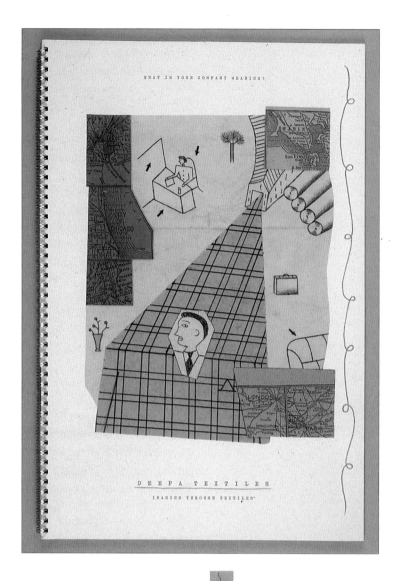

WHAT IS YOUR COMPANY WEARING?

D E E P A   T E X T I L E S
IMAGING THROUGH TEXTILES®

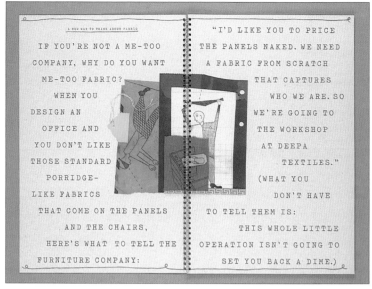

IF YOU'RE NOT A ME-TOO COMPANY, WHY DO YOU WANT ME-TOO FABRIC? WHEN YOU DESIGN AN OFFICE AND YOU DON'T LIKE THOSE STANDARD PORRIDGE-LIKE FABRICS THAT COME ON THE PANELS AND THE CHAIRS, HERE'S WHAT TO TELL THE FURNITURE COMPANY:

"I'D LIKE YOU TO PRICE THE PANELS NAKED. WE NEED A FABRIC FROM SCRATCH THAT CAPTURES WHO WE ARE. SO WE'RE GOING TO THE WORKSHOP AT DEEPA TEXTILES." (WHAT YOU DON'T HAVE TO TELL THEM IS: THIS WHOLE LITTLE OPERATION ISN'T GOING TO SET YOU BACK A DIME.)

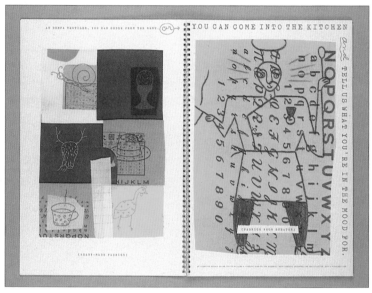

AT DEEPA TEXTILES, YOU CAN ORDER FROM THE MENU. OR YOU CAN COME INTO THE KITCHEN and TELL US WHAT YOU'RE IN THE MOOD FOR.

{READY-MADE FASHION}

Design Firm:
Michael Mabry Design,
San Francisco, California
Art Director/Designer:
Michael Mabry
Illustrator:
Philippe Weisbecker/
Riley Illustration

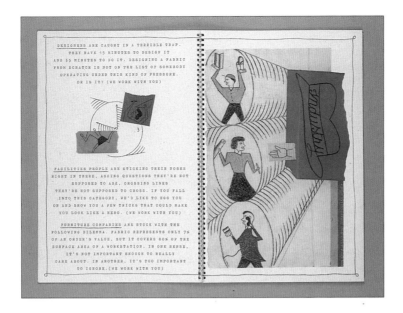

Deepa Textiles designs office furniture fabric "for companies who know who they are," according to its trademarked slogan. Michael Mabry Design's oversized (11" x 17"), wire-bound booklet featuring the whimsical collage drawings of Philippe Weisbecker charmingly captures the spirit of a small company that "is in the business of addressing the appalling emptiness and lack of soul of the American office." The naive quality of the drawings, printed on a thick, warm, slightly speckled stock, creates the impression of extremely personal service. Two pages of drawings represent the company's employees. The amusing copy, printed in a typewriterish font, reinforces the personal message, claiming that "each company deserves its own solution, not a borrowed one."

DEEPA TEXTILE CO.

Design Firm:
Copeland Hirthler
Design+Communications,
Atlanta, Georgia
Creative Directors:
Brad Copeland,
George Hirthler
Designers:
Melanie Bass,
David Woodward
Illustrators:
Fredrik Broden, Jerry
Burns, Mark Shelton
Copywriters:
Melissa James Kemmerly,
Marti Nunn

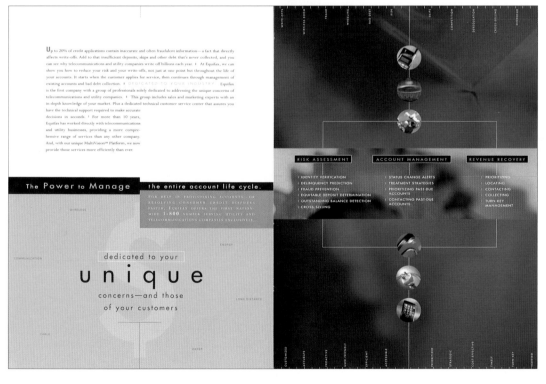

When Equifax wanted to advertise its financial services to a new market comprised of the telecommunications and utilities industries, it turned to Copeland Hirthler Design+ Communications for "new market" brochures that would work within the company's existing collateral imaging system. Copeland Hirthler sought to produce something with elegant, executive appeal, yet enough technical information to satisfy hands-on managers. The majority of the design budget went to photography, which has been added to Equifax's custom library of images for future consistency and cost efficiency. All the components of the cover image, for example, were supplied separately on film to make it easy to incorporate these elements into future pieces. The cover image establishes a visual metaphor for Equifax's relationship with telecommunications and utilities clients, while the introductory pages address the problems facing managers in these markets. The rest of the 9" x 12 1/2" brochure is devoted to outlining Equifax's capabilities and services, and the back cover incorporates a pocket folder to hold more specific divisional and product information. Additional collateral materials include product brochures, direct mail campaigns, and under-the-door pieces for trade shows.

SHR PERCEPTUAL MANAGEMENT

SHR Perceptual Management brand and corporate identity consultants promotes its services to major firms with this plastic spiralbound booklet, covered in Classic Columns Marigold. Housed in a stiff black slipcase with a die-cut grab space that reveals the SHR logo when the booklet is pulled out, the piece measures 8 1/2" x 14". End papers in Classic Columns Red Pepper echo the color of the logo. Designed in-house, the substantial booklet was intended to create an understated business image through high-impact visuals, describing an approach to the shaping of perceptions using as few words as possible. Text and product images are printed on white Karma, much of which is left blank. While the spreads feature small-scale photographs, four gatefolds expand selected images to double-page size. The book-like approach was selected to separate the piece from the brochure masses, and to make it more difficult to throw in the "circular file."

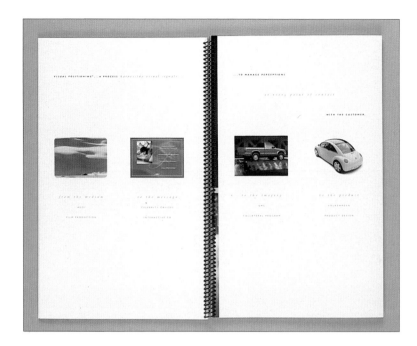

Design Firm:
SHR Perceptual
Management,
Scottsdale, Arizona
Art Director:
Barry Shepard
Designer:
Karin Burklein Arnold

Design Firm:
The Impact Group,
Snowmass Village,
Colorado
Art Directors:
Scott Paramski,
Sean Patrick
Designer:
Scott Paramski
Photographers:
Gerry Kano, Tom Ryan,
Bill Westheimer,
B. Ross DeSciose
Copywriter:
Sean Patrick

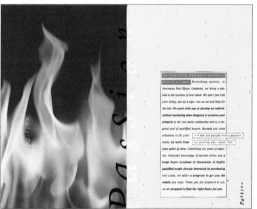

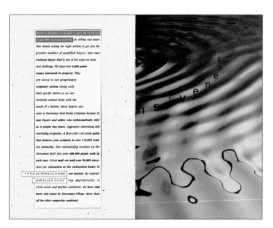

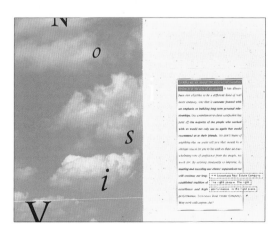

Snowmass Real Estate Company, with over 25 years of experience in the Aspen/Snowmass market, positions itself as an experienced and environmentally-conscious firm with these 6" x 9 1/2" fold-out brochures for its "Elements" campaign, designed by The Impact Group. Abstracted images of mountains, clouds, fire, and water are printed in 4-color process on Mohawk Superfine to achieve a vibrant duotone effect. The visuals represent the company's "elements of success": strength, vision, passion, and responsiveness. The photos were both commissioned and stock, to achieve cost-consciousness and visual coherence. Pull-out cards inserted in the brochures feature an element image on one side, with a photo and a personal statement from a Snowmass salesperson on the other.

SNOWMASS REAL ESTATE COMPANY

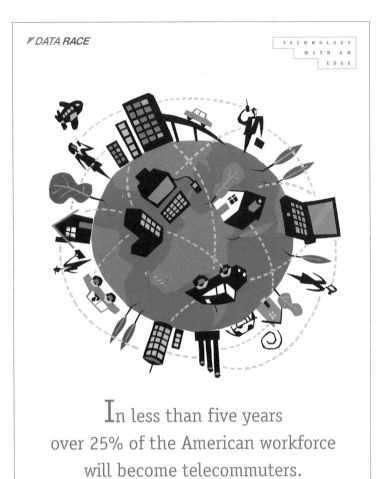

Design Firm:
Peterson & Company,
Dallas, Texas
Art Director/Designer:
Scott Ray
Illustrator:
Craig Frasier

The future belongs to those who have the best access to the corporate information environment.

In today's information driven economy, a quality product and good service no longer guarantee business success. The ability to change quickly has become equally important. And the information to make quick and accurate decisions must be instantly available. To stay competitive in this volatile new marketplace requires a whole new set of strategies, plus a greater appreciation for the role that information technology can play in a company's success. Things change so rapidly now, that without immediate access throughout your organization to the latest and most accurate information, your company could quickly find itself out of the running.

The World has Changed.

Today's most competitive companies are those that are best equipped to share and exchange a full range of information: internally with co-workers, and externally with vendors and customers. With immediate access to essential business knowledge, decisions can be made quickly from anywhere in the world. It becomes much less important where a company's

home office is located, or where its employees work. What matters instead, is the ability to always stay a few steps ahead of the competition. In this environment, access to information can become the critical differentiator. The company that can react the fastest to market changes and new customer demands has the competitive edge.

In today's global economy you must be able to make decisions anywhere.

Stay ahead of your competitors with immediate access to your corporation.

At DATA RACE, our business is to provide your company with the tools to succeed in today's information driven economy. We are an innovator and world leader in providing remote access to the corporate environment. DATA RACE has already achieved a solid reputation with our ability to create innovative and unique communications solutions that challenge all existing ground rules. We are re-defining business communications with products that include the world's only line of custom OEM modems offering integrated voice capabilities, a full duplex speaker phone, telephone answering machine, fax answering and much more. Additionally, we offer a revolutionary new approach to remote branch office multiplexing, with a product line based on a unique multiprocessor design that ensures your investment won't become obsolete as new technologies such as ISDN, ATM, T1/E1 and Frame Relay become available.

Building a foundation for an information driven economy: why DATA RACE has the edge.

None of the products we make is an end in itself. They are modular building blocks that can be used to build a total communications solution. Our mission is to provide complete, integrated access to the corporate information environment. By offering the world's most advanced notebook computer modems and a flexible new open systems approach to remote office multiplexing, DATA RACE has established a firm foundation for continuing our leadership role in providing the information solutions that business needs to succeed in an information-based economy.

To reach new clients—half of them non-tech people—custom fax modem and "multiplexing" systems manufacturer Data Race requested a brochure that was different from the industry standard, something fun to look at and easy to understand. Peterson & Company responded with a colorful, uncluttered piece that communicates with pictures rather than technobabble. Craig Frasier's Photoshop illustrations translate complex networking technologies into friendly, people-and-planet oriented, organic systems. Printed in offset 6-color on Mohawk Superfine, the 9" x 12" brochure incorporates a die-cut pocket for inserts inside the back cover.

Design Firm:
Willoughby Design Group,
Kansas City, Missouri
Art Directors/Designers:
Michelle Sonderegger,
Ingred Fink
Copywriter:
John Jarvis

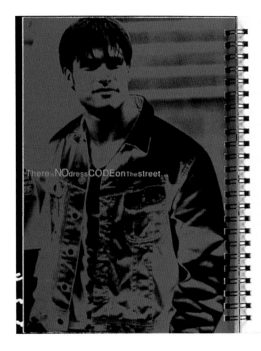

Lee Apparel wanted to reposition itself for a more youthful audience with an image piece emphasizing friendship, romance, and three key clothing concepts: Urban, Retro, and Natural. Willoughby Design developed a small (6 1/8" x 8 5/8"), spiralbound booklet, enlivened with inserts and gatefolds, for distribution to the fashion traders, as well as television and movie production companies. Commissioned photographs and illustrations (including pieces by artists better known for their Hallmark greeting cards work) depict very attractive young people in Lee clothing. Postcards, notepads, paper dolls, and booklets-within-a-booklet create an "interactive" effect. A perforated page opens up to reveal a poster; and a featured pair of vintage jeans, shown front and back, were embroidered hippie-style in 1975 by the sister of one of the designers—their mother had preserved them for the past 20 years.

When Cutler Travel Marketing, planners of incentive and corporate group travel, asked Sayles Graphic Design to overhaul their corporate identity, the mandate was to produce something fun, not slick and high-tech. After developing a global icon illustrated in Sayles's retro style, the design firm created a small, inexpensive "introduction" brochure, as well as this easily-customized follow-up booklet (measuring 6" x 7 1/2"). Interior pages, printed on Curtis Tuscan Antique, alternate calendar sheets with company information and customer testimonials.

Interspersed among these are blank pages onto which custom travel memorabilia from around the world can be attached: coins, stamps, postcards, maps; even doo-dads like miniature serapes and drink stirrers. All the art decorating the interior pages and the chipboard cover was hand-rendered by John Sayles, and no computers were used for the project.

Design Firm:
Sayles Graphic Design, Inc., Des Moines, Iowa
Art Director/Designer/Illustrator:
John Sayles

Design Firm:
Nesnadny+Schwartz,
Cleveland, Ohio
Creative Directors:
Mark Schwartz,
Tim Lachina
Designer:
Tim Lachina
Illustrator:
Tim Lewis
Production:
Mark Schwartz
Copywriter:
The Henry Woodward
Company
Printer:
Fortran Printing, Inc.

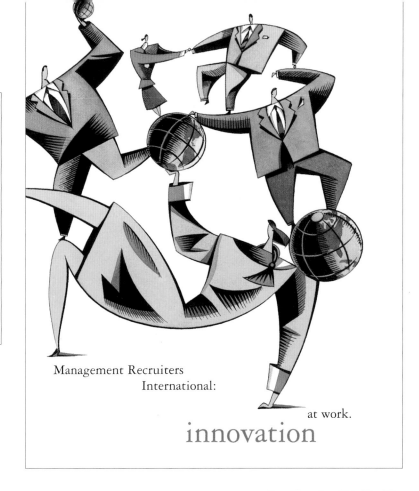

Management Recruiters
International:

at work.

innovation

diversity.

The future is here

and has a smile on its face.

OfficeMates5 Today's technology requires an office support staff more flexible, capable, and knowledgeable than ever before. OfficeMates5 locates, evaluates, and recommends people with the training, talent, and personality to make your office work more efficiently.

DayStar DayStar is the answer for managers who need talented support staff to meet variable staffing challenges. We identify the very best and train them in today's office technology. DayStar will change the way you think about temporary services.

technology.

We take the information superhighway

to work every day.

ConferView MRI created the largest videoconferencing network (over 100 cities) in the world to save our clients substantial amounts of time and money when interviewing candidates for key positions. Visit New York in the blink of an eye (and you don't have to go through LaGuardia).

DBsky and Data-on-Demand Our computer-linked database gives MRI search professionals instant access to millions of industry-specific candidates.

MRI University Only MRI regularly conducts multi-location, interactive, video-based distance education. Our search professionals are the best educated and informed specialists in the world.

The MR/SC Selection System The most advanced assessment technology helps you thoroughly evaluate prospective employees' potential fit with your company, before you make them a job offer.

Vision on Video MRI's own video studio and production facilities have made MRI professional training programs the envy of the staffing industry.

MRIware We developed the most versatile search-industry information system in the world. Exceptional information management helps us deliver extraordinary results.

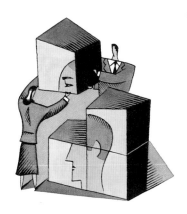

Management Recruiters International, in its attempt to be "the world's preferred and pre-eminent provider of human resource solutions," looked to Nesnadny+ Schwartz for a brochure that would break new ground in marketing communication through the use of highly conceptual, original illustrations. Commissioned from Tim Lewis, the images provide visual metaphors for key concepts like "vision," "innovation," and "diversity." They are accompanied by a minimal text (written by The Henry Woodward Company), for an effect that is elegant but not cold. The entire "Innovation" brochure, which measures 9" x 11 $^1/_2$", is printed on S.D. Warren Lustro Dull.

MANAGEMENT RECRUITERS INTERNATIONAL

Design Firm:
Group One Creative/
Brown Shoe Co.,
St. Louis, Missouri
Art Director/Designer:
Courtney Walker
Illustrator:
Donna Mehalke
Copywriter:
Laney Glenn

LARRY STUART/BROWN SHOE COMPANY

Retail sales associates and store buyers of Larry Stuart shoes are introduced to the new "Essentials" line for women through this 7" x 7" brochure, designed in-house by Group One Creative, Brown Shoe Company. Because the latex-soled "Essentials" shoes combine comfort with casual elegance, the brochure needed to communicate a similar message, as well as provide concrete selling suggestions. Black-and-white wash draw-

ings of women and shoes by Donna Mehalke provide fashionable visuals. Printed on roughly textured black, white, and red Strathmore Grandee pages, the images of women are punctuated by stripped-in red lips. Though produced with a very small budget, the brochure fits into a black slipcase with a die-cut that displays the "Essentials by Larry Stuart" name.

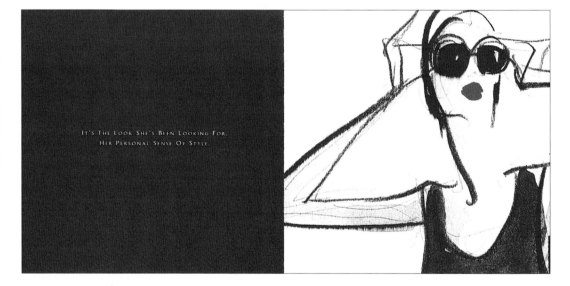

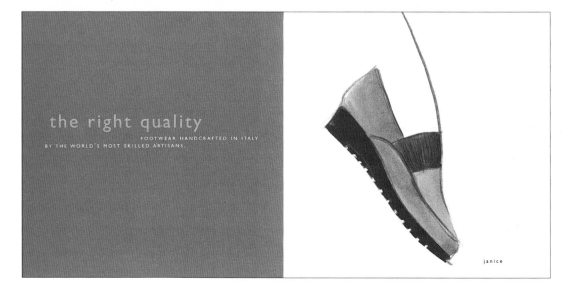

Design Firm:
Ison Design,
Santa Ana, California
**Art Director/Designer/
Illustrator:**
Paul Ison
Photographer:
Peter Samuels
Copywriter:
Dawn Hylton Gottlieb
Agency:
The Wilshire Group

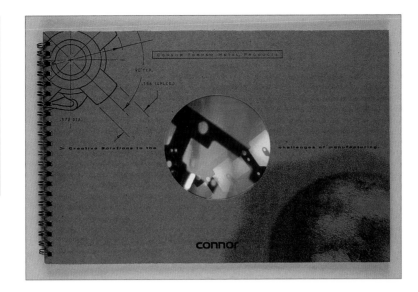

In this piece, the client wished to reposition itself from a "bid-by-job" formed metal supplier to a strategic partner for world-class companies. Ison Design's brochure emphasizes how employee-owners drive "The Connor Process." The first half of the horizontal (11 1/2" x 7 3/4") wire-o bound booklet opens with a history of the company and a timeline including financial numbers. A gatefold spread matches final products like computer monitors and IV pumps to specific Connor metal parts. A two-gatefold spread diagrams "The Connor Process" from "challenge" through "evaluation." The second section focuses on "real people solving real problems" by interspersing short pages depicting employees (shot in black-and-white and colorized in Photoshop) overlaid with personal comments between abstracted photo-illustrations. A glimpse into the design process of one particular part is displayed through short pages that show its evolution. In total, five stocks are used in the book.

CONNOR FORMED METAL PRODUCTS

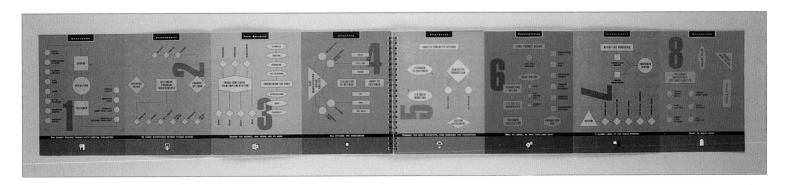

Brochures and booklets aimed at recruiting the best and brightest young people into the corporate world need to take into consideration that, whatever their post-commencement career plans, most students still live in an MTV world. The two sets of recruiting literature shown here—for Andersen Consulting, by Mobium Creative Group (pp. 30–31); and Booz Allen & Hamilton, by Belk Mignogna Associates (this spread)—rely on illustration to welcome students to the "real world" without overwhelming them with the corporate experience. Both design firms developed recruiting literature in the form of a series of booklets, to divide the information into easily comprehensible units—explaining what their client does, or how one's career will progress, for example. These booklets are supplemented with small black-and-white photos showing the clients' employees. The Booz Allen & Hamilton recruiting literature is contained within a die-cut folder that also holds a writing pad, while an interactive CD-ROM is given out with the Andersen Consulting materials.

To reach the top MBA students from the world's leading business schools, management consulting firm Booz Allen & Hamilton hired Belk Mignogna Associates to create a distinctive recruitment package. The "Face to Face" system includes five different-sized brochures detailing company information from "The Work" to "The Global Opportunities." A folder pocket holds the brochures in a stepped arrangement that displays a continuous image printed across their covers. These brochures and a writing pad are held within a larger (9" x 12") folder with a custom die-cut flap closed with velcro buttons. The illustrations linking the folder and brochures were commissioned from José Ortega, while graphs resembling Dada collages were created by Belk Mignogna Associates.

Design Firm:
Belk Mignogna Associates Ltd., New York, New York
Art Director:
Steve Mignogna
Designers:
Bazil Findlay,
Michelle Marks,
Donna Dornbusch
Illustrator:
José Ortega

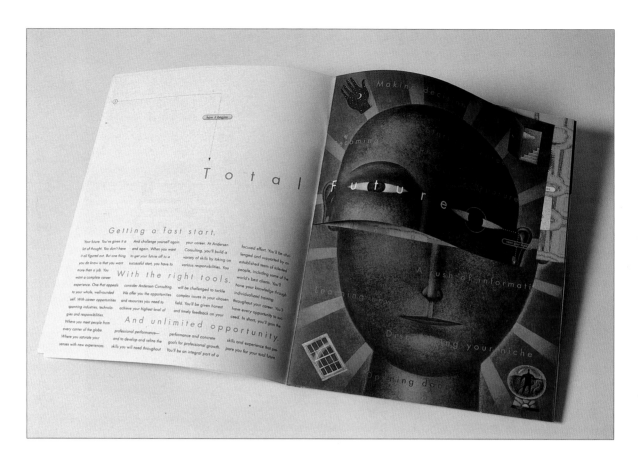

Design Firm:
Mobium Creative Group,
Chicago, Illinois
Creative Director:
Guy Gangi
Art Directors:
Tom Bell, Jerzy Kucinski
Illustrators:
Raul Colon, John Kleber,
Tom Curry, Kathy
Gendron, Joel Nakamura,
Mitch O'Connell
Copywriter:
Dawn Williams Bertuca

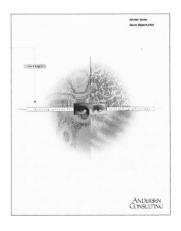

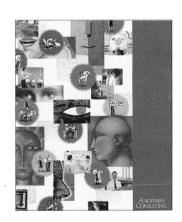

For a new system of recruiting literature, Andersen Consulting, a division of Arthur Andersen & Company, sought something that would appeal to the college audience of the '90s. Mobium Creative Group complied with "Total Future," a brochure that combines illustrations of faces with Photoshop-enhanced video stills featuring company employees to emphasize the human aspect of the recruiting process. Details of images commissioned from six illustrators are combined on the cover, while each illustration is employed whole for a separate spread. The top half of the image is printed on a half-sheet. The reader is encouraged to "open your mind" by lifting the half-sheet, under which is found a timeline graph representing "the first week of training" or "the first two years." This "interactive" feature is reinforced by a CD-ROM that is distributed with the 9" x 11 1/2" brochure, along with supporting literature that can be tucked into a folder pocket inside the back cover.

ANDERSEN CONSULTING

Increasingly, companies feel the need to reassure their customers that they are behaving responsibly toward the natural environment. In both of the external report pieces featured here—Central and South West System's "Measuring Up" environmental report, by John Flaming Design (p. 34); and "The Coca-Cola Company and the Environment," by Sibley/Peteet Design (p. 35)—extremely simplified, silkscreen-like illustrations and easily legible graphs and charts are utilized to demonstrate environmental awareness. Both reports are printed in sans-serif fonts, to suggest accessibility, and on uncoated stock—recycled, of course. The third piece for distribution to external audiences shown here, KPMG Health Care & Life Science's "Blueprint for Building the Biotechnology Business" (this spread), though not specifically about the environment, employs natural motifs and images like leaf icons and photographs of trees to make its point about "growing" its industry. Designed in-house, the booklet uses the metaphor of constructing a tree-house to represent its message.

Design Firm:
KPMG Design,
Montvale, New Jersey
Art Director/Designer:
Donna Bonavita
Illustrator:
Nicholas Wilton

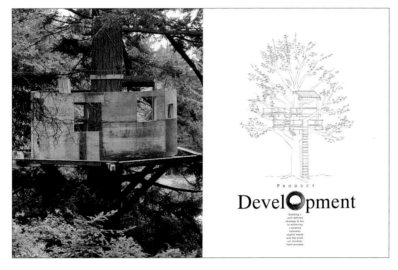

PRODUCT

Devel**O**pment

Building a
well-defined
strategy is key
to achieving
a balance
between
capital needs
and the prod-
uct develop-
ment process.

HEALTH ECONOMICS

The **Climb** FROM DRUG COST
TO DRUG VALUE

KPMG produced this
8 1/2" x 11" brochure,
"Blueprint for Growth:
Building the Biotechnology
Business," in-house in three
weeks. (The illustrations,
commissioned from Nicholas
Wilton, had to be turned
over in eight days.) To reach
an audience including
investment bankers, ana-
lysts, and venture capitalists,
as well as the CEO's and
senior executives of biotechnology companies, the
design team developed a
central motif of a treehouse,
which is repeated in illustrations, photographs, and
graphs and charts constructed from wood and wood-
working tools. Color separa-
tions were made using fre-
quency-modulated screen-
ing for more detail than conventional 200-line screens,
and blueprint and rice paper
illustrations were direct
scans. Because the text is
dense, main points are out-
lined in the margins in
brown ink, and information
for specific groups (emerg-
ing, mid-tier, and top-tier
employees) is keyed with
icons such as an acorn and
an oak leaf.

The Central and South West System provides electrical service to almost 4.3-million people in the southwestern U.S. In order to demonstrate environmental compliance to its shareholders, the company inaugurated an environmental report, created in 1994-1995 by Jon Flaming Design and Newman Graphics. The 6" x 9" booklet, printed on Simpson Evergreen, resembles a field journal, with loosely set text, suggestive of an office memo. Full-page illustrations that metaphorically represent Central and South West System employees safeguarding the environment are supplemented with colorful charts and small diagrams of company equipment.

Design Firms:
Jon Flaming Design,
Newman Graphics,
Dallas, Texas
Art Directors:
Jim Foley, Jon Flaming
Designer/Illustrator:
Jon Flaming

13

Renewable Energy Project
The CSW system's Renewable Energy Project near Fort Davis in West Texas is a form of intensive practical research which includes a wind farm, a

There are environmental advantages derived from renewable energy sources, (but) some environmental impacts ... must be considered.

solar park and several independent solar applications. The power generated by the solar park and wind farm will be connected to West Texas Utilities Company's electrical grid and will supplement the Fort Davis power supply. The study will track the reliability of each system and factor the results into the system's overall power generation strategy.

Independent applications include solar-powered street lights, warning signs, irrigation and water-pumping systems in remote areas and rooftop photovoltaic (PV) systems. These can be seen in Marfa, in and around Fort Davis and at Sul Ross State University in Alpine.

These renewable energy sources are dependent on either sun or wind. It is expected that these technologies will supplement traditional fossil fuel, nuclear and hydroelectric generation, but they are not ready to equal the traditional fuels' around-the-clock, year-long reliability.

Anemometers at our wind farm measure wind speed and, along with a package of other instruments. Wind direction, air temperature and rainfall.

SOLAR POWER
Though there are environmental advantages derived from renewable energy sources by avoiding air and water emissions, there are also some environmental impacts that must be considered. A solar park requires a large land area in order to generate a significant amount of electricity. Land devoted to solar generation prevents other land use or development as little will grow in the panels' shade and neither wildlife nor livestock can use the land.

22

The task force is currently in the process of developing a baseline for PCB risk exposure with respect to equipment type, location and PCB content. Each operating company is faced with differing regulations and pressures regarding PCB usage.

Although the EPA retains regulatory control of equipment in use, it allows individual states to set standards for PCB spill cleanup and PCB-contaminated material disposal. As a result, Texas and Louisiana have implemented more restrictive standards for PCB cleanup.

MINE RECLAMATION
Surface mining still has a reputation for land abuse. "Strip" mining, as it is sometimes still known, in the past removed whatever was of value and left open trenches and mounds of earthen debris. The Surface Mining Control and Reclamation Act of 1977 changed those old practices. Today, after mining and reclamation, the land is left contoured and at least as productive as it was before mining. In 1994, the South Hallsville and Dolet Hills mines together produced 6.1 million tons of lignite. This mining affected 1,112 acres, but 1,203 acres were reclaimed for a variety of uses. (We reclaimed more acreage than was disturbed last year because acreage placed in temporary cover the previous year was converted to permanent cover.)

Post-mine land use and the types of vegetation planted are determined by the landowner, who usually request commercial forest, pasture and grazing land. In 1994, we reclaimed 606 acres of commercial forest, 267 acres of pasture and 246 acres of grazing land. Eighty-four

23

acres were converted to wildlife habitat and wildlife food plots were added to an additional 52 acres.

Electric and Magnetic Fields
The emphasis on electric and magnetic field (EMF) research shifted to occupational studies with 1994's Canadian-French study and 1995's Savitz study. Occupational studies offer several advantages, including a workforce that possibly has the most consistent and intense exposure, accessible medical records and exposures that can be reasonably reconstructed. The results, however, have been like earlier residential studies — inconsistent and inconclusive.

The CSW system continues to support EPRI's research to determine if health effects are associated with low-level exposure to EMF.

While fewer inquiries indicate interest in the EMF issue has declined in the past year, we continue to remain current with the research and answer our customers' concerns.

Occupational Health
In last year's Environmental Report, we described the recent expansion of our Occupational Health/Industrial Hygiene program and its centralization in our Dallas corporate headquarters. We are now realizing the benefits of our efforts.

We expect to have the first of two phases of our systemwide, computerized Material Safety Data Sheet (MSDS) program on-line this year. This program improves our ability to track chemicals and manage exposures to them. We expect to enter more than 10,000 MSDSs, each averaging two to three pages of data. The "keyword-search" function will enable employees to access the correct data sheet by the chemical's exact or partial name.

Land Uses After Reclamation 1994

Air Quality
CSW's electric operating companies use 103 active generating units capable of producing 14,316 megawatts of electricity. A diverse fuel mix is used to fire the boilers, including natural gas (47 percent in 1994), coal (38 percent), lignite (9 percent) and nuclear (6 percent). In addition, one small hydroelectric plant in South Texas accounts for a fraction of a percentage point.

Considerable effort goes toward removing ash particles from the exhaust gases of those plants fueled by coal or lignite. Electrostatic precipitators handle the dirty work, and do so at an average efficiency rating of 99.75 percent. An electrostatic precipitator (ESP) is a series of electrically charged wires and plates. The ESP is located in the exhaust gas stream between the boiler and stack or chimney, where all the exhaust must pass over them. The fly ash particles are pulled to the charged surfaces much like a person's hair is attracted to a brush or comb on a dry day. The ash is removed from the wires and plates and periodically taken from the collection hoppers for disposal.

CSW's coal and lignite plants produce approximately 1.3 million tons of fly ash. Of this, little more than 3,000 tons escape into the atmosphere, which is less than Environmental Protection Agency (EPA) and state permits allow.

SO_2 Reduction
Our lignite and some coal plants use "scrubbers" to remove sulfur dioxide (SO_2) from exhaust gases. Scrubbing is a chemical process that uses calcium carbonates found in limestone. Limestone is pulverized to a fine powder, mixed with water and sprayed into the flue gas stream. The calcium carbonate reacts with the sulfur released by coal combustion to form a calcium sulfite sludge. This

CSW 1994 Fuel Mixture

Fly Ash Captured VS. Released

Design Firm:
Sibley/Peteet Design,
Austin, Texas
Art Director/Designer:
Rex C. Peteet
Illustrators:
Rex C. Peteet, K.C. Teis

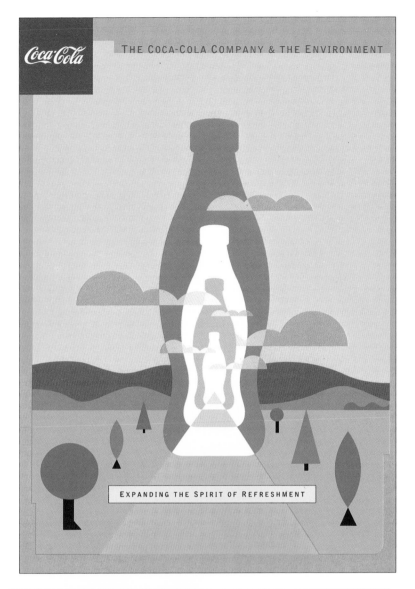

To inform concerned consumers about Coca-Cola's environmental policies and practices, the international beverage firm distributes this "Expanding the Spirit of Refreshment" piece, designed by Sibley/Peteet. Because the information had to be accessible and appealing to a wide audience, the graphics were kept simple. Soy-based inks and recycled stock were employed for the 7" x 10" brochure, of course, and inexpensive print production was necessary to enable mass distribution. Screen specifications were considerably compensated (30 to 40 per cent in some instances) for use on uncoated Georgia-Pacific paper so ink saturation on solid areas would not be compromised. An unusual touch is a yellow half-sheet listing Coca-Cola's environmental policies that is die-cut into the classic Coke bottle shape.

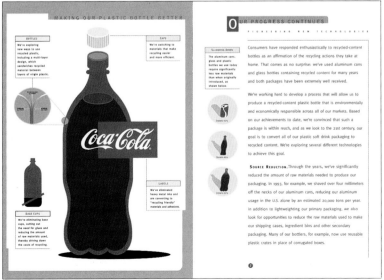

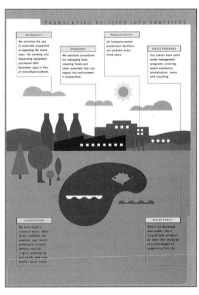

THE COCA-COLA COMPANY

While the reports for internal distribution within two companies shown in this section serve very different purposes, they are both constructed around conceptual illustration. A booklet outlining "values, principles, and guidelines" for the employees of Pacific Telesis (p. 38), designed by Luxon-Carrá with illustrations by Jeffrey Fisher of Riley Illustration, is simple and direct—black-and-white text and images, with red headlines for contrast. Fisher's drawings are friendly, yet reinforce the notion that company employees are expected to "uphold the highest standards of ethical conduct in all of our business activities." "Many Beginnings, One Singular Adventure: The Astra Merck Story" (this spread), created by Acme. A Marketing Design Group, needed to do two things: relate the history of the pharmaceutical company from a business point of view, and capture the energy and enthusiasm of some of the many individuals who helped to shape the company. The two parts of the book are unifed through conceptual illustrations (by three different artists) and photographs of the people involved.

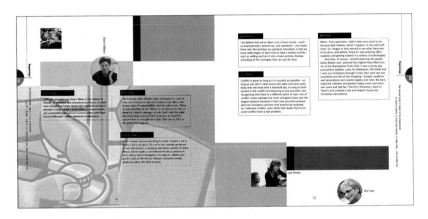

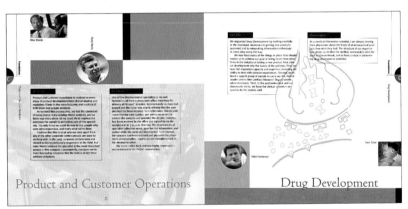

Design Firm:
Acme. A Marketing and
Design Group,
Newton, Pennsylvania
Art Director:
Charles Reed
Designer:
John Mulvaney
Photographers:
Peter Olson, Michael
Slack, Steve Coan
Illustrators:
Chris Gall, Nicholas
Wilton, Eric Grahl,
Tom Curry
Copywriter:
Beth Kephart Sulit
Production Assistant:
Erinn Kenney
Production Company:
MJM Creative Services,
Inc.

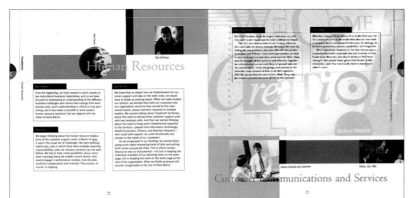

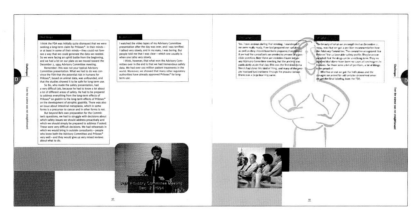

"Many Beginnings, One Singular Adventure: The Astra Merck Story" was commissioned by the start-up joint venture pharmaeutical company and its business building consultant and partner, Andersen Consulting, as a one-year anniversary gift to thank those who assisted in building the company. The 8" x 8" booklet employs black-and-white photographic portraits of employees, archival stills which form duotone backdrops for text, and video still frames. The video stills were digitized and brought into Photoshop, where a custom filter was applied in order to give them a raster-line effect. Commissioned illustrations, interspersed with pre-existing company graphics, represent key concepts. This wide range of visual material and a text that combines history and personal interviews are held in place with a loose, shifting grid composed of De Stijl-like strips of color. Part one of the book, which tells the Astra Merck story, is printed on an uncoated, colored recycled sheet to support text-heavy areas and the reproduction of tritones. Part two, which features key employees, utilizes a dull white premium sheet, chosen to enhance the 4-color imagery while achieving optimum contrast between ink and paper surface.

The Pacific Telesis employee handbook, designed by Luxon-Carrá, succeeds in conveying the communications firm's "values, principles, and guidelines" in a serious and attractive fashion. Because Pacific Telesis wanted something that would deliver employee regulations in an engaging, accessible way, Luxon-Carrá employed a limited palette (black, white, gray, and red), simple typography, and whimsical yet informative black-and-white drawings commissioned from Jeffrey Fisher. Section headlines are printed in an attention-getting red ink, while the main text is done in gray. Areas deserving special attention or reiteration are printed in a bold black face, and issues regarding company security are further emphasized by a rule. The entire brochure (measuring 8 3/4" x 11 1/4") is printed on Simpson Evergreen, and the back cover incorporates a pocket folder.

Working at Pacific Telesis

Values, Principles, and Guidelines
For Employees of
Pacific Telesis Group Companies

Effective March 1995

Design Firm:
Luxon-Carrá,
New York, New York
Art Director:
Mark Coleman
Designer:
Hiroki Asai
Illustrator:
Jeffrey Fisher/
Riley Illustration

1 Upholding Our Principles

People often form opinions about a company based on just one experience with a single employee. Your actions—either directly or indirectly—can influence the way the public views Pacific Telesis Group.

We believe that you have both a right and responsibility to understand what we expect of you as a representative of the corporation. The aim of this handbook is to clarify those expectations. It outlines applicable laws and provides general standards for appropriate practices at Pacific Telesis Group companies, whether on corporate premises or while engaged elsewhere in corporate business.

Administration and Enforcement

We expect supervising managers (known as *coaches*) to administer and enforce our corporate standards. Toward this objective, all coaches should:

• Ensure that each employee receives and reads a copy of this handbook, and signs and returns a copy of the Acknowledgment Certificate.

• Emphasize to employees that they can report activities believed to violate our standards or applicable legal regulations without fear of reprisal.

• Develop standards and procedures that comply with corporate policies and any applicable legal regulations.

As an employee, whether supervisory or non-supervisory, you also should:

• Comply with all principles and guidelines contained in this handbook.

• Comply with both the letter and spirit of all federal, state, and local laws and regulations that apply to our business.

• Be familiar with and adhere to any additional policies and practices that are specific to your company or department.

Whenever you need further guidance, information, or immediate assistance, there's someone available to help. Just call the appropriate contact listed on the sheet in the back pocket.

Working at Pacific Telesis 1995 | 1

RETAIL SALES

Designers of retail sales brochures are usually allowed a bit more leeway for fun than those working on corporate communications—but rarely do they get to take it as far as the firms responsible for promoting Timex/Joe Boxer watches and O'Brien International Watersports equipment. Not only did Smart Design produce a brochure/poster to offer a new line of Timex/Joe Boxer watches, but they got to create the watches themselves, in "goofball" Joe Boxer style. O'Brien, too, wanted something that emphasized its irreverent attitude, and The Leonhardt Group complied with a catalog that needs to be read every which way, including upside-down, which seems to be a position that the O'Brien customer is not uncomfortable in—at least on waterskis.

Other firms find their mandate is to produce a sales brochure that is warm and welcoming, but still serious. This seems to be an especially effective approach when one's budget for imagery is limited, as was the case for the Sundog travel gear catalog and for a brochure used to introduce Nike's F.I.T. fabrics. Hornall Anderson revitalized already-existing line drawings of Sundog products through additional drawing and airbrushed overlays. Printed on uncoated, recycled stock, the catalog also suggests environmental responsibility. Nike likewise colorized stock imagery from its archives to illustrate its F.I.T. brochure, promoting weatherproof fabrics. Herman Miller's "Response 10" brochure, while projecting an image of computer-aided efficiency for this new quick-ship program, introduces the complexities of contract furniture to mid-sized businesses with accessible graphics and text. Printed in a limited palette on an uncoated

stock, it evokes efficiency without being too slick.

Brochures for car sales, while ostensibly featuring a great piece of machinery, and certainly embellished with engineering diagrams, often foreground a car's emotional appeal. Saatchi & Saatchi Pacific, in a brochure for Toyota, used visuals like lightning, racing helmets, and Grand Prix tickets to assert the "personality" of the "racebred" Supra. The Designory, on the other hand, sought a more abstract yet still emotional appeal in its brochures for Mercedes-Benz of North America's SL-Class cars. Images of the cars set in beautiful locations alongside attractive people suggest that to step into a Mercedes SL-Class automobile is to step into a world of romance and elegance.

Elegance is also key for some of the fashion and accessories brochures and catalogs shown here, but it's an elegance taken to an arty—even surreal—extreme. Vanderbyl Design's catalog for Robert Talbott Neckwear intersperses Ansel Adams–like landscape photos among the more expected (and equally gorgeous) shots of neckties and bowties. A brochure for Maramara Millinery Design, by Segura Inc., places obviously hip (and sometimes tattooed) contemporary women in hats in sepia-duotones evocative of an era when the well-dressed woman never went out without her chapeau. And Geof Kern's haute couture fashion photos for Neiman Marcus magazine inserts depict stunningly-clad models in settings like fractured narratives: Why is she looking at jewelry offered by a strange man in an alley? Why are they hiding their faces behind linens on a clothesline? And why is she stuck to that shrub?

In this group of brochures, promoting retail clothing and accessories sales, fashion and funkiness are employed in both expected and unexpected ways. Vanderbyl Design's booklet for Robert Talbott Neckwear (this spread) says "elegance" from start to finish, from the gold type on the cover to the gold threads woven into the magnificent ties featured in the spreads. Segura Inc.'s small brochure for Maramara Millinery Design (p. 43) also suggests elegance, but in a "downtown," hip kind of way, with its out-of-focus photos of chic and tattooed young women in Maramara hats. The men's clothing depicted in a magazine insert for Neiman Marcus stores, done in-house, is similarly funky (pp. 44–45)—but in a very high-fashion way, as befits the designers depicted (Prada, Versace Jeans Couture, etc.). On the other hand, the sensibility for the Neiman Marcus women's designer-clothing insert is high fashion taken to the point of surrealism (pp. 46–47), with a model as likely to be suspended in midair or standing giant-size over a tiny village as posing by a tree or on the seashore. Some of the Timex watches in an accordion-fold poster/brochure by Smart Design (p. 42) are surreal as well, such as the one that offers 13 instead of 12 hours, but the happy (watch) face-filled, black, white, and yellow piece is pure silliness.

Design Firm:
Vanderbyl Design,
San Francisco, California
Designer:
Michael Vanderbyl
Photographer:
David Peterson

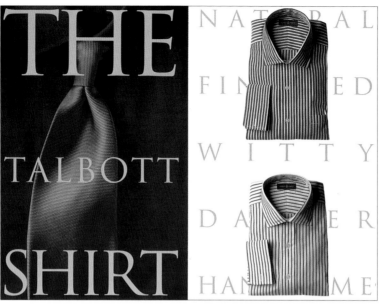

ROBERT TALBOTT
NECKWEAR REMAINS
THE MOST ELEGANT OF
GENTLEMEN'S ACCESSORIES:
HANDSOME, WELL-MADE AND QUITE
AFFORDABLE. THE UNSURPASSED QUALITY OF
ROBERT TALBOTT NECKTIES BESPEAKS TRADITION
AND REFINEMENT, A QUIET ASSURANCE WITH REMARKABLE
POWERS OF SUGGESTION. FROM THE SPIRITED CLASSICS OF THE
BEST OF CLASS COLLECTION TO THE AUDACIOUS PRINTS OF OUR
EXCLUSIVE OMAGOLD SERIES, TALBOTT OFFERS AN ARRAY OF SUPPLE

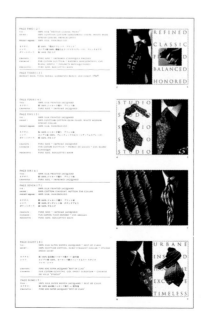

REFINED

CLASSIC

FINED

BALANCED

HONORED

PASSION

BALANCE

PRESTIGE

HERITAGE

LUXURY

"Robert Talbott Neckwear remains the most elegant of gentlemen's accessories," begins the gold-printed, all-caps text running across the cover of a catalog done for the Carmel, California menswear studio by Vanderbyl Design. The gold caps carry the message of elegance and "unsurpassed quality" throughout the book's text, drawing out shades of gold in the gorgeous neckties and bowties shown alone and in combination with equally beautiful shirts, vests, and jackets. The catalog text explains that the "magnificent beauty of rock, sea and cypress drew Robert Talbott to Carmel and perhaps inspired the tapestry of of color that he sought in silk." The incredibly rich, fabric-laden spreads are punctuated by four muted photographs of austerely beautiful rock formations and mountains. The 7" x 11" catalog is printed on Mead coated papers.

ROBERT TALBOTT, INC.

The theme of this Timex brochure is the happy (watch) face, and that's what Smart Design employees are wearing after creating a Joe Boxer line of watches and the brochure to promote them. Timex wanted something that could serve as a take-away poster (it opens to a 46 1/2" width), yet be small enough to fit on the countertop in the store as a brochure (folded, it measures 3" x 9 3/4"); something that would convey necessary information (including "hidden messages" that appear when the Indiglo function is used) to retail buyers and salespeople. It also had to appeal to the consumer as a souvenir, and the watches had to be shown actual size. The accordion fold, using 100-lb. Monadnock Astrolite Smooth Text, allowed for all these requirements. And Joe Boxer's "goofball humor" was of prime importance, as can be discerned from the text, with lines like this, about the "waistband" watch: "Think of it as a jock strap for your wrist."

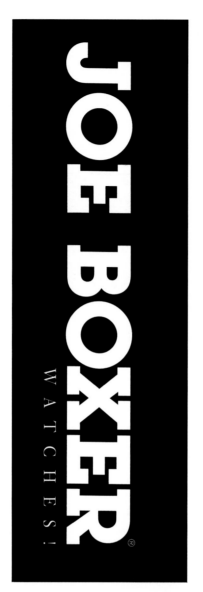

WALL STREET
blk 03635 $50

Are you a big-shot, wheeler-dealer, or tycoon? If you live in the world of high finance, then this is a must for your watch portfolio. It gives you advice you can't buy on The Street.

BLIND DATE
brn 03636 $50

Cheaper than a tarot-card reading and just as accurate. This visionary watch predicts your future — as long as it's Good, Bad, or Ugly.

03636

Design Firm:
Smart Design Inc., New York, New York
Art Director:
Tucker Viemeister
Designers:
Debbie Hahn, Stephanie Kim, Nick Graham/Joe Boxer

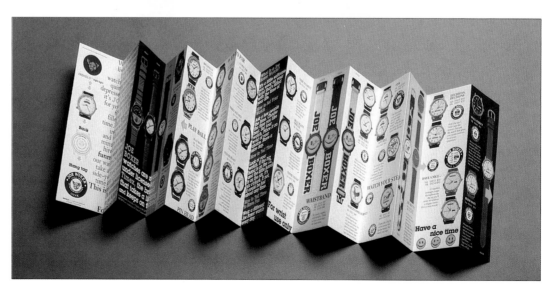

Design Firm:
Segura Inc.,
Chicago, Illinois
Art Director/Designer:
Carlos Segura
Photographer:
Jeff Sciortino

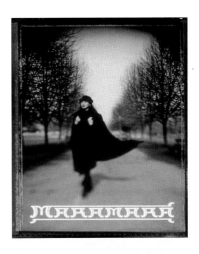

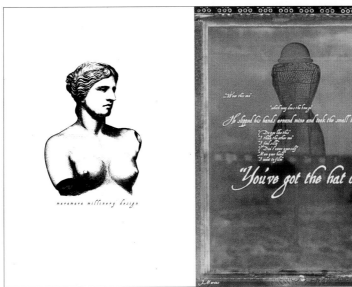

This $5000 brochure for Maramara Millinery Design, makers of hand-made hats, doubles as a promotion for Segura Inc.; Segura's type foundry, [T-26]; photographer Jeff Sciortino; and Mead Signature Gloss, the stock used. Sciortino's sepia duotones focus mainly on the hats, and only sometimes on the faces—and tattoos—of their models. The flourishes of Jim Marcus's font, Aquiline, add to the retro-elegance of the photos. The catalog text, written by Anna McCalister and printed in white over full-page images, poetically treats the experience of hat-wearing rather than providing traditional catalog fare. The brochure measures 5 1/2" x 8 1/4".

MARAMARA MILLINERY DESIGN

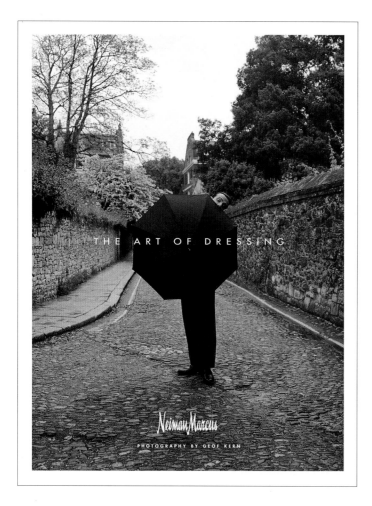

THE ART OF DRESSING

Neiman Marcus

PHOTOGRAPHY BY GEOF KERN

DOLCE & GABBANA

GIANNI VERSACE

Neiman Marcus

VERSACE CLASSIC

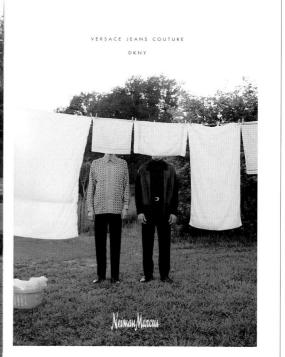

VERSACE JEANS COUTURE
DKNY

Neiman Marcus

MISSONI

INDUSTRIA
ANTHONY TARASSI

NeimanMarcus

CALVIN KLEIN COLLECTION

NeimanMarcus

CK CALVIN KLEIN

The main task facing the Neiman Marcus advertising team in the creation of these brochures for insertion in fashion magazines was to differentiate the merchandise from the surrounding editorial pages and ads, while uniting pieces by numerous designers with a consistent Neiman Marcus theme. Photographer Geof Kern was hired for his style and vision, which in this case took a surrealistic turn. He conceived two high-fashion brochures—"The Art of Dressing," featuring men's attire, and "The Art of Fashion," for women's clothing. Both were shot in Devon, England, where, art director Georgia Christensen reports, the locals were "delightful and extremely cooperative." The faces of the male models in "The Art of Dressing" (this spread) are often obscured—behind an umbrella, an outstretched arm, or a blindfold; eyes closed in sleep; even replaced by a bouquet of red roses in full bloom. "The Art of Fashion," on the other hand (see following spread), features one model, depicted on the cover dreaming about being a high-fashion model. In her dream, then, she is flying through the trees, stuck to a hedge, walking giant-sized through a tiny village, even carried along as if she were literally a mannequin— while wearing Chanel, Prada, Versace, and so on.

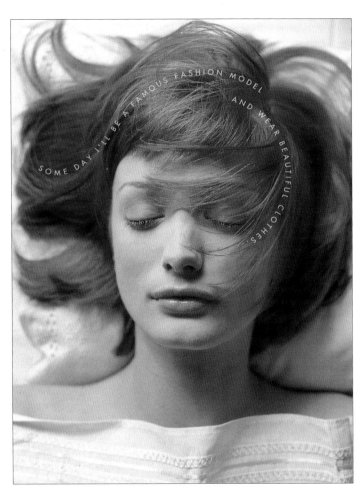

SOME DAY I'LL BE A FAMOUS FASHION MODEL AND WEAR BEAUTIFUL CLOTHES

Design Firm:
Neiman Marcus
Advertising, Dallas, Texas
Art Directors:
Georgia Christensen,
Bob Robertson
Designer:
Georgia Christensen
Photographer:
Geof Kern
Copywriter:
Amy Adams

LAGERFELD

MOSCHINO COUTURE!

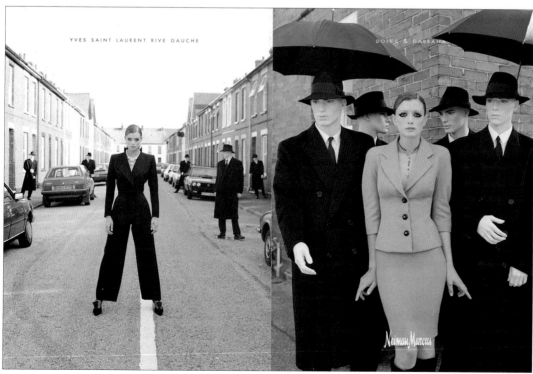

YVES SAINT LAURENT RIVE GAUCHE

DOLCE & GABBANA

The three sports equipment and clothing brochures seen here present three different sensibilities: scientific, wacky, and eco-friendly. To educate consumers about a new line of fabrics for sports clothing, Nike went with a "scientific" approach (this spread), using photos of environmental conditions and diagrams to explain how the different F.I.T. fabrics keep wearers cool and dry. In-store, a display resembling a chemical experiment accompanied the brochure. In a catalog for O'Brien International's 1996 water-ski product line—"100% Hardcore," as it says on the cover—The Leonhardt Group stayed with the O'Brien company line (p. 51). Spreads are run sideways, charts upside down, and goofy bits of advice are offered, alongside photos of people doing wild things on O'Brien equipment, and color shots of the products—design statements in themselves. A catalog for Sundog travel gear, on the other hand, takes a subdued, eco-friendly approach, limiting photography to the cover, while using line drawings to represent the products inside (p. 50). The Sundog catalog, designed by Hornall Anderson, was printed on uncoated stock, as were the booklets for O'Brien and Nike.

Design Firm:
Nike Inc.,
Beaverton, Oregon
Art Director/Designer:
Dan Richards
Copywriter:
Stanley Hainsworth

DRI-F.I.T. IF YOU WORK OUT, YOU'RE GOING TO SWEAT. BUT ARE YOU STILL GOING TO STAY COMFORTABLE? **SWEAT IS GOOD. BUT, TOO MUCH AND YOU'LL OVERHEAT OR GET CHILLED. DRI-F.I.T.** MICROFIBER FABRIC WORKS TO KEEP YOU COMFORTABLE — TRANSPORTING PERSPIRATION FROM YOUR SKIN TO THE OUTSIDE FOR RAPID EVAPORATION. WORKOUT. SWEAT. STAY COMFORTABLE. NOTHING PERFORMS BETTER.

THERMA-F.I.T. YOU CAN WEAR ALMOST ANYTHING TO STAY WARM. BUT CAN YOU STILL MOVE? **WHEN YOU WORKOUT IN THE COLD YOU NEED TO STAY WARM, BUT YOU STILL WANT FREEDOM OF MOVEMENT. THE TIGHT KNIT OF THERMA-F.I.T.** FLEECE WORKS LIKE A MICROFIBER BLANKET — EXTREMELY WARM, LIGHT AND COMFORTABLE. LIGHTWEIGHT FREEDOM FROM THE COLD. NOTHING PERFORMS BETTER.

When Nike created this brochure to educate consumers about the technical features of their F.I.T. fabrics and to establish a graphic identity for the category, they needed to create something that would fit into a retail display and include a business reply card, without spending any money on new photography. Visuals from the Nike image bank were printed as duotones to represent the four types of environmental conditions to which the four types of fabric correspond, and four graphic symbols were also developed. While the photographic images are based on square units, echoing the shape of the 5 1/4" x 5 1/4" brochure, the symbols are circular, and the brochure's text repeats their red, white, and black colors and sans-serif caps. The entire brochure was created in Quark XPress and printed on Simpson Evergreen. The brochures were supported in-store by a "chemistry experiment" display.

NIKE INC.

Hornall Anderson's mandate in designing a new Sundog mail-order catalog was to create a more upscale image for the travel gear company while working within an extremely limited budget. To this end, the design firm recycled line drawings from an earlier catalog, touching them up with cross-hatching in the foreground, drawing over lines for textural effect, and adding white airbrushed overlays to enliven the product images when printed. The product pages were printed in black and white on a recycled paper, gray Genesis Fossil Script, and enclosed in a four-color, double-gated Teton Cover Tiara White sheet featuring warmly-lit product photographs by Darrell Peterson. Editorial comments were handwritten in script to suggest a travel journal, and the product descriptions are done in a typewriter font. Some pages have underprints of natural elements like shells, leaves, and pine cones, to underscore the company's commitment to the environment.

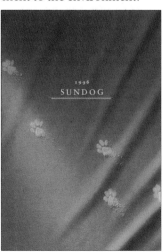

Design Firm:
Hornall Anderson
Design Works,
Seattle, Washington
Art Director:
Jack Anderson
Designers:
Jack Anderson,
David Bates
Illustrator:
Todd Connor
Photographer:
Darrell Peterson
Copywriter:
Julie Huffaker

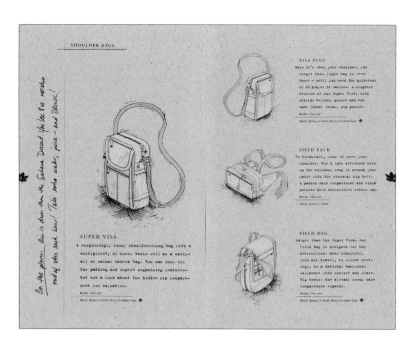

Design Firm:
The Leonhardt Group,
Seattle, Washington
Designers:
Mark Popich, Allen
Woodard, Melissa
Gustafson
Illustrator:
Mark Popich
Photographers:
Doug Dukane, Tom King,
Dan Taylor, Don Mason

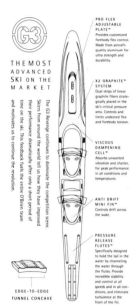

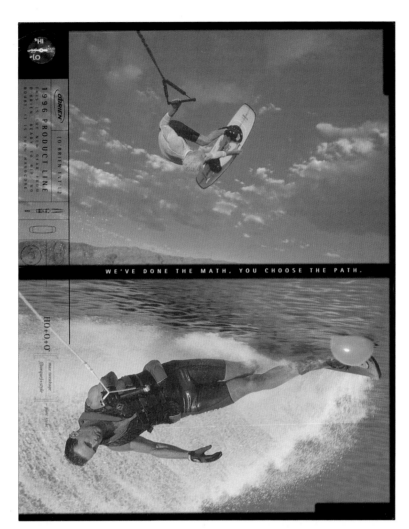

WE'VE DONE THE MATH. YOU CHOOSE THE PATH.

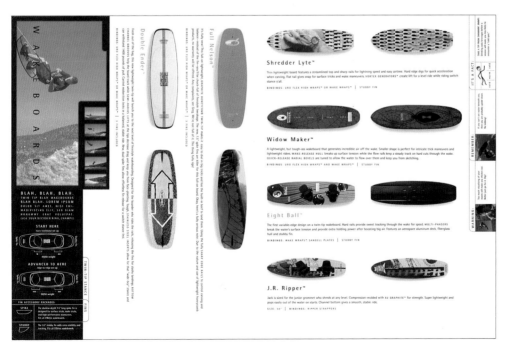

While it was important that the O'Brien International Watersports catalog highlight the merchandise and its technical strengths, its main subject is the pursuit of fun. The Leonhardt Group approached the project with tongue-in-cheek humor, with the aim of capturing O'Brien's irreverent attitude by titling a blank section of the back page "gratuitous ad space," or incorporating wise bits of information like "If you can't see water beneath you, then you are probably upside down." The imagery combines the client's product shots with in-action photos of O'Brien water skiers art-directed by Mark Popich, the Leonhardt Group designer. Spreads alternate between horizontal and vertical formats, with charts (serious and not) printed along the sides, or even upside down at the top of the page. A generous amount of white space, in combination with saturated surf colors, gives the 8 1/4" x 11" catalog a clean, crisp look.

Though both are designed to sell office equipment, the two pieces presented here couldn't be more different. Michael Orr and Associates went for a classically corporate look in their gatefold inserts for The Gunlocke Company (this spread). Austere yet richly detailed photographs are focused solely on the chairs being offered, for maximum appeal to the serious business client. The inserts can be easily organized, updated, and customized. The brochure for Herman Miller's "Response 10" program ("Out our door 10 days after you place your order") has an entirely different feel (pp. 54–55). Instead of detailing products, photographs are employed to show furniture in different office environments, in some cases being used. Specific office components are represented in drawings, along with schematic diagrams giving floor dimensions. The different design approaches in these two brochures are also evident in the papers and types used: The Gunlocke inserts are printed on stiff, glossy stock, with traditional, subdued type, while the Herman Miller booklet, printed on a lightweight, uncoated paper, features a specially-designed font created to evoke a digitally-aided, fast and efficient "response."

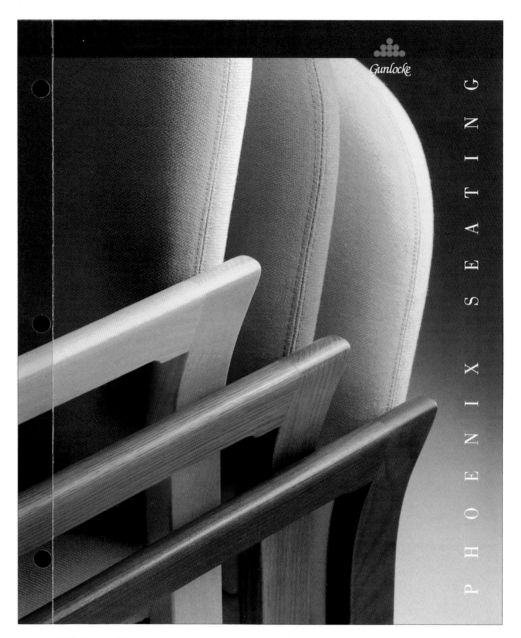

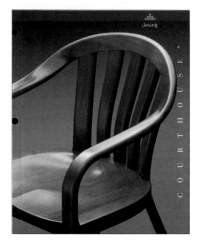

To best reach its clients—specifiers and purchasers of contract furniture—The Gunlocke Company looked to Michael Orr and Associates for a well-organized, high-quality literature system. Orr produced a series of gatefold 8 3/4" x 11" inserts, printed on a stiff LOE 80-lb. Cover, to be held in three-ring binders for ease in client customization and product updates. The product is shown in detail on the outer page of the gatefold, which, when opened, reveals complete images of product variations, as well as a short text printed in white. (Some gatefolds open to a three-page spread.) The back of each insert offers details such as colors and suggested uses, as well as schematic drawings of the models and their dimensions. Photographs from company archives were employed, and Scitex was used to change some wood and fabric colors, avoiding the need for new photography.

Design Firm:
Michael Orr & Associates,
Inc., Corning, New York
Art Director:
Michael R. Orr
Designer:
Gregory Duell
Photographer:
Myers Studios

RESPONSE 10™ PROGRAM

Out our door 10 days after you place your order

FROM HERMAN MILLER

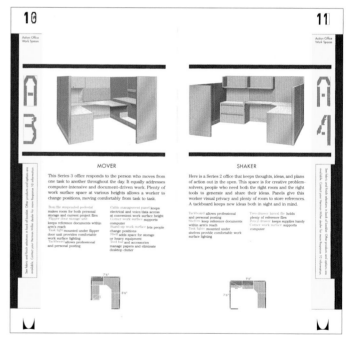

MOVER

This Series 3 office responds to the person who moves from one task to another throughout the day. It equally addresses computer-intensive and document-driven work. Plenty of work surface space at various heights allows a worker to change positions, moving comfortably from task to task.

Box/file suspended pedestal makes room for both personal storage and current project files
Flipper door storage unit keeps reference documents within arm's reach
Task light mounted under flipper door unit provides comfortable work surface lighting
Tackboard allows professional and personal posting

Cable management panel keeps electrical and voice/data access at convenient work surface height
Corner work surface supports computer
Stand-up work surface lets people change positions
Shelf adds space for storage or heavy equipment
Tool bar and accessories manage papers and eliminate desktop clutter

SHAKER

Here is a Series 2 office that keeps thoughts, ideas, and plans of action out in the open. This space is for creative problem-solvers, people who need both the right room and the right tools to generate and share their ideas. Panels give this worker visual privacy and plenty of room to store references. A tackboard keeps new ideas both in sight and in mind.

Tackboard allows professional and personal posting
Shelves keep reference documents within arm's reach
Task light mounted under shelves provide comfortable work surface lighting

Two drawer lateral file holds plenty of reference files
Pencil drawer keeps supplies handy
Corner work surface supports computer

Ethospace
Work Spaces

S Y S T E M S

Stopping at nothing short of rethinking and redefining the elements and structure of office architecture, Designers Bill Stumpf and Jack Kelley delivered the Ethospace system. It's a whole new kind of product that breaks the traditional panel system down into smaller elements. Steel frames and tiles work together to build sturdy three-and-a-half-inch-thick walls that create an impression of architectural permanence. Frames and tiles can be updated, resurfaced, or reconfigured easily, quickly, without special tools, and with minimal disruption to work in progress. These frames host the most versatile and easily altered energy and cable management features in the industry.

Our Response 10 Ethospace workstations feature many of the tile types that give the Ethospace system its flexibility. We've designed these offices to take advantage of the neat cable management features that help technology-driven offices keep current.

But if you don't find exactly what you need, your dealer can help. With three frame heights, a stacking frame, and face, acoustical, tackable, cable access, glazed window, open, and rail tiles, you can build and rebuild an Ethospace office however, whenever you want.

Some Tile Options

Tackable   Cable Access   Open   Rail

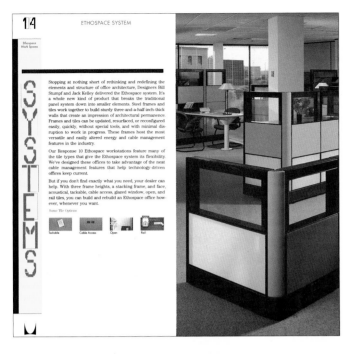

ACTION OFFICE FABRICS

F A B R I C S

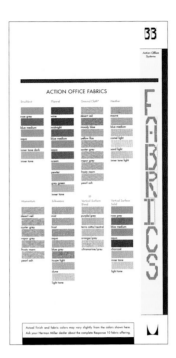

Actual finish and fabric colors may vary slightly from the colors shown here.
Ask your Herman Miller dealer about the complete Response 10 fabric offering.

Ergon 3 Chairs

C H A I R S

This is the latest advancement of the Ergon® chair, the very first ergonomic work chair, designed by Bill Stumpf and introduced in 1976. Ergon chairs have supported millions of office workers around the world. And now Ergon 3 chairs build in greater performance with enhancements that help meet the needs of an evermore diverse work force. Three sizes of Ergon 3 chairs support a broad range of physical types—large and small, tall and short, male and female. New sizes, adjustable arms, and other features enhance the chair recognized for its familiar profile of thick, waterfall cushions.

Work Chair Options

Three sizes: a, b, or c
Knee tilt with or without forward angle adjustment
Back angle or no back angle adjustment

Adjustable arms, fixed arms, or no arms
Hard casters for use on carpet or soft casters for use on hard floors

See fabric and finish selections in back of booklet. Other products and options are available. Contact your Herman Miller dealer for more Response 10 information.

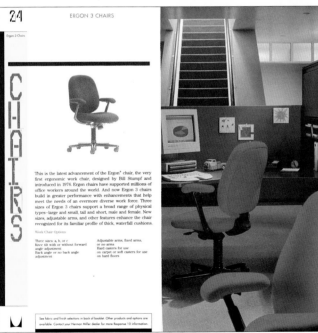

Design Firm:
Herman Miller, Inc.,
Zeeland, Michigan
Art Director/Designer:
Kevin Budelmann
Copywriter:
Julie Ridl
Photographer:
Nick Merrick

Herman Miller's "Response 10" brochure, describing a new quick-ship program for office furniture, needed to be a self-contained direct-mail piece that could be used easily by Herman Miller dealers in their local markets. Because the intended audience of mid-sized businesses is not always familiar with the complexities of contract furniture, the brochure also had to introduce workplace issues such as ergonomics, workstyle preferences, and technology support with accessible graphics and language. And, the unit cost to the dealer per piece had to come in under one dollar. The need for an uncoated paper that would be smooth enough to accept 4-color process imagery well and that would be light enough for mailing yet sufficiently opaque within the budget requirement led to the selection of Simpson Satinkote. The 5 1/2" x 11" brochure features a color palette of black, white, gray, yellow, and red, with FreeHand illustrations with mezzotint effects from Photoshop. Some lighting effects were also created in Photoshop. In addition, the designer developed a brochure-specific bit-mapped typeface to convey fast, efficient overnight service.

HERMAN MILLER INC.

Though cars are above all pieces of fast-moving technology, they are sold as much for their emotional appeal as their engineering, and the automobile brochure is a primary way to establish that appeal. Brochures for Mercedes-Benz's SL-class cars, created by The Designory (this spread), are built around not only the expected questions, like "What makes a Mercedes-Benz a Mercedes-Benz?" but also more romantic queries, like "Where will your desires drive you?" Loaded with images of beautiful people and exotic places, along with cars parked in gorgeous settings or literally streaking through the landscape, the implied answer is: into the lifestyles of the rich, young, and discreetly famous. A brochure for the 1996 Toyota Supra, produced by Saatchi & Saatchi Pacific (pp. 58–59), combines sharp-focus car shots, grainy images that set a mood (a still life of a leather jacket, sunglasses, a Toyota cap, and Grand Prix tickets), and precise cutaway engineering illustrations, set on generously sized pages.

Dreams

Mercedes-Benz SL-Class

Imagine

Inspiration

Desires

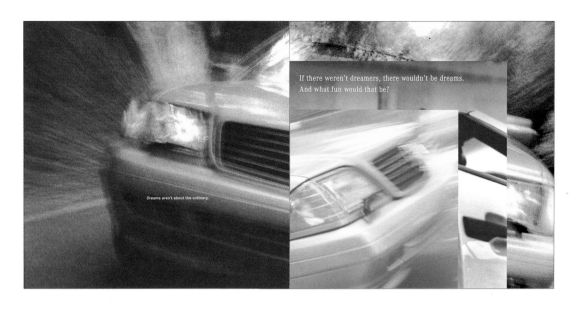

If there weren't dreamers, there wouldn't be dreams.
And what fun would that be?

Dreams aren't about the ordinary.

This four-brochure campaign for Mercedes-Benz of North America's SL-Class cars, created by The Designory, Inc., emphasizes a more youthful attitude for the venerable automotive company while maintaining its traditional brand image. Mercedes wanted to present its cars in an emotionally appealing way, accomplished through spreads depicting the line's fun-to-drive qualities alongside information about engineering, safety, performance, and comfort. In keeping with the need to attract a younger audience, stress is placed upon the environmentally-friendly aspects of Mercedes, including waterborne car paints. The variously sized brochures themselves were printed on a Zanders recycled gloss paper containing a minium of 25 per cent pre- and postconsumer waste, developed specifically for Mercedes-Benz. And for the technologically aware, a two-diskette program that allows the viewer to study a Mercedes from the outer finish to the drivetrain, also by The Designory, can be slipped into the back pocket of the brochures.

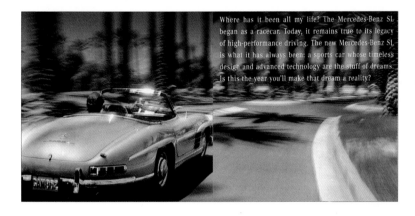

Where has it been all my life? The Mercedes-Benz SL began as a racecar. Today, it remains true to its legacy of high-performance driving. The new Mercedes-Benz SL is what it has always been: a sports car whose timeless design and advanced technology are the stuff of dreams. Is this the year you'll make that dream a reality?

Design Firm:
The Designory, Inc.,
Long Beach, California
Creative Director:
Tim Meraz
Art Director:
Andrea Schindler
Photographers:
Harry DeZitter, Tim
Damon, Charles Hopkins,
Thomas Heinser
Copywriters:
Richard Conklin, Dalin
Clark, Christopher
Hoffman, Viki Nicols

Antilock Braking (ABS), Traction Control and the new Electronic Stability Program (ESP). All SL-Class models are equipped with two critical safety features designed to maintain driving stability in dynamic situations. ABS helps prevent the wheels from locking during braking, so the driver can retain steering control on slippery surfaces. Traction control systems help keep the drive wheels from slipping during acceleration. And for 1996, the SL500 offers you ESP, a new active-safety option that automatically helps to correct oversteer or understeer while cornering.

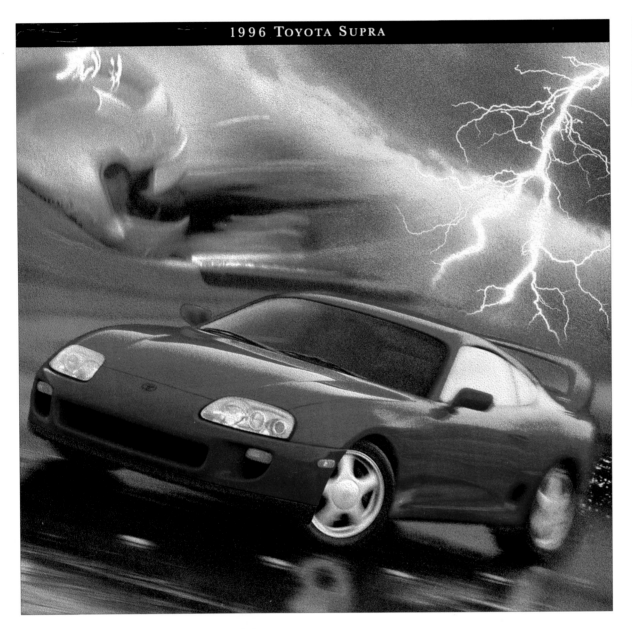

1996 TOYOTA SUPRA

Agency:
Saatchi & Saatchi Pacific,
Torrance, California
Creative Director:
Dean Van Eimeren
Art Director:
Bob Rome
Designer:
Karen Knecht
Illustrator:
Kevin Hulsey
Photographer:
David LeBon

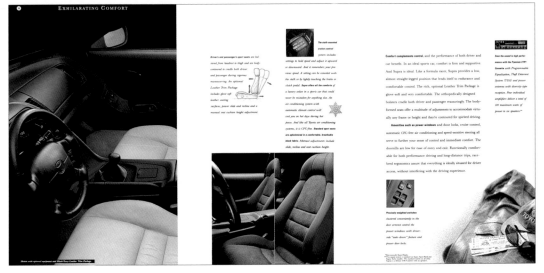

Toyota's annual brochure budget runs to over $10 million. In creating this brochure for the Toyota Supra, Saatchi & Saatchi Pacific needed to achieve a balance between a book worthy of a premium product and the limited quantities premium products actually sell. To capture the "personality" of the "race-bred" Supra, a cover photograph portraying the car, a helmet (to convey serious intent), and lighting (to symbolize power and attitude) was manipulated with noise filters in Photoshop and output from an Iris printer before color separation to achieve a grainy effect. Inside the brochure, technical cutaway illustration communicates the car's world-class technology and refined dynamics. A generous size (11" x 11") and gatefolds assist in conveying the Supra's appeal and technical performance information within a very limited number of spreads, since extravagant page counts are difficult to justify in the dwindling sports car market. Other than red touch plates to augment red car photos and dull varnish on the white of each page, printing (on Vintage Remark) was straightforward.

Although mechanical equipment is displayed in the booklets featured in this section, distinctly human elements were emphasized by the designers of the pieces. The "Rain Bird Field Report," created by Nordensson Lynn Advertising to showcase Rain Bird landscape irrigation spray heads (this spread), has a binding made of twine, and the first page displays telltale coffee-cup rings. A typewriter font, hand-drawn sketches with notes, ink-and-watercolor cutaway diagrams, and amusing "Polaroid" inserts (Old Faithful labeled "Not quite as bad as Audra spouting off back at the office") effectively convey the company's message of "superior craftsmanship, advanced application of technology, and innovative solutions to irrigation problems" in a friendly way. Simantel Group's brochure for Caterpillar Industrial Products (p. 64) solves the problem of depicting their custom components without showing the machines that other companies use them in by illustrating hypothetical machines around photographs of CIPI components. The colorful, almost fine-art images add warmth to a mechanical subject, as do photographs of Caterpillar employees at work. Samsung's calendar (pp. 62–63), by Addison Design Company, caricatures famous inventors whose findings influenced the development of the kinds of products offered by the Korean manufacturer.

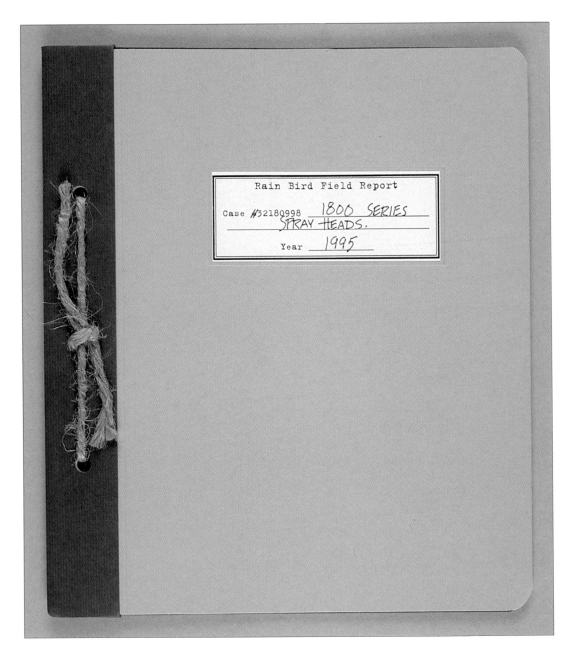

Agency:
Nordensson Lynn
Advertising,
Tucson, Arizona
Creative Directors:
Scott Timms,
Phillip Smith
Designer:
Pam Stone
Illustrator:
Bob Conge
Copywriter:
Mike Nevin

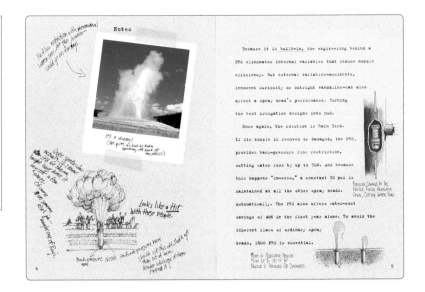

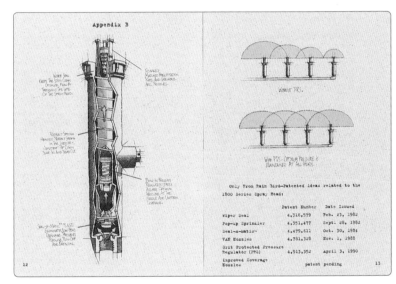

Rain Bird Sales looked to Nordensson Lynn Advertising to produce a booklet that would re-establish its 1800 Series landscape irrigation spray heads as the premier name plate in the category, despite intense competition and a maturing market. Because the target audience—landscape architects—is typically inundated by direct mail, the brochure had to be distinctly different. To set Rain Bird apart, and to ensure that the product will be remembered, Nordensson Lynn designed an 8" x 9 1/2" brochure that resembles a field report, enlivened with "rewards" for the reader like twine binding, humorous drawings by Bob Conge, taped-in "Polaroids," and paper-clipped notes. The text combines hand-written comments and a typewriter font. To carry out Rain Bird's slogan, "Conserving more than water," the hand-assembled 1800 Spray Head brochure was printed with "environmentally responsive" dryography on recycled papers: Champion Benefit (cover), Simpson Quest (interior), and Simpson Evergreen Kraft (mailing envelope).

RAIN BIRD SALES, INC.

DMITRI MENDELEYEV
(1834-1907)

A Russian chemist, Mendeleyev is known for formulating the Periodic Table which explains the relationship between elements by listing them in order of their atomic weight. Although elements with similar properties appeared at regular intervals, there were gaps in the table. To Mendeleyev, these empty spaces represented elements that had not yet been discovered. In 1886 one of his predictions became a reality when ekasilicon (renamed germanium), an element with semiconducting properties, was discovered.

S	M	T	W	T	F	S
	1	2	3	4	5	6
7	8	9	10	11	12	13
14	15	16	17	18	19	20
21	22	23	24	25	26	27
28	29	30	31			

Produced by Samsung Semiconductor, the 256M DRAM chip is the result of a $150 million investment, can store the data contained in a 40-volume encyclopedia and promises to become the core technology in multimedia and high-definition TV.

JANUARY 1

SAMSUNG

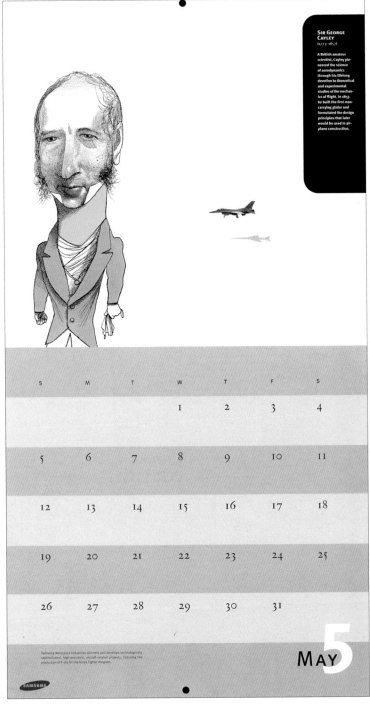

SIR GEORGE CAYLEY
(1773-1857)

A British amateur scientist, Cayley pioneered the science of aerodynamics through his lifelong devotion to theoretical and experimental studies of the mechanics of flight. In 1853 he built the first man-carrying glider and formulated the design principles that later would be used in airplane construction.

S	M	T	W	T	F	S
			1	2	3	4
5	6	7	8	9	10	11
12	13	14	15	16	17	18
19	20	21	22	23	24	25
26	27	28	29	30	31	

Samsung Aerospace Industries pioneers and develops technologically sophisticated, high-precision, aircraft-related projects, including the production of F-16s for the Korea Fighter Program.

MAY 5

SAMSUNG

Design Firm:
Addison Design
Company,
New York, New York
**Creative Director/
Art Director/Designer:**
Dan Koh
Illustrator:
John Springs
Printer:
Samsung

YOUNG-SIL CHANG
(Late fourteenth century - early fifteenth century)

Young-sil Chang was a scientist during Korea's Chosun Period (1392-1910) who made devices to measure astronomical phenomena. His most famous invention was a Gyok Ru, a sophisticated water clock which he completed in 1434. Mr. Chang studied Chinese and Arabian water clocks and then expanded on those ideas to create a unique, improved design.

S	M	T	W	T	F	S
1	2	3	4	5	6	7
8	9	10	11	12	13	14
15	16	17	18	19	20	21
22	23	24	25	26	27	28
29	30	31				

Samsung Watch products are designed for practicality and beauty. The special gold plating is virtually scratch-proof. The watches maintain their accuracy to within 20 seconds per month and have proven water-resistant in demanding underwater tests from 30 to 200 meters (98 to 656 feet).

DECEMBER 12

SAMSUNG

SAMSUNG

Samsung manufactures everything from batteries to double-hulled tankers, and this "Salute to Inventors" calendar, by Addison Design Company, uses humor to combine some of the greatest minds in history with the company's latest technological products: Samuel F.B. Morse with an extremely compact plain-paper fax machine; Leo Baekeland (inventor of plastic) with Ecophil, a biodegradeable resin product; mathematician Charles Babbage with a Pentium notebook PC. Caricatures are supplemented with product photos to create the illustrations, with explanatory text limited to black insets. Through the 11 3/4" x 11 1/2" calendar, Samsung reaches a global business community through an amusing format that underscores the company's mission to create new, superior products that provide lasting benefits.

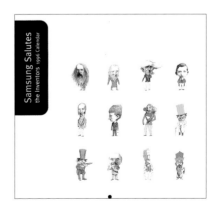

Samsung Salutes
the Inventors 1996 Calendar

CATERPILLAR INDUSTRIAL PRODUCTS

CIPI (Caterpillar Industrial Products, Inc.) is a wholly-owned subsidiary of Caterpillar Inc., designer and manufacturer of earth-moving, construction, mining, and material equipment, as well as diesel engines. To advertise that CIPI can provide and incorporate custom components for other manufacturers' machines and equipment, the Simantel Group designed this 8 1/2" x 11" brochure. The main visual problem involved depicting CIPI components without showing machines made by other companies. The solution was to integrate photographs of the CIPI pieces within illustrations of complete machines, as if they might be imagined during a design phase. (The photographs—commissioned, stock, and existing cient photos—and commissioned illustrations were combined in Scitex at the color separator.) The resulting images suggest that anything can be achieved using Caterpillar components.

Design Firm:
Simantel Group,
Peoria, Illinois
Art Director:
Jim R. Jones
Illustrator:
Ken Clubb
Photographer:
Rick Kessinger

CATERPILLAR® INDUSTRIAL PRODUCTS, INC.

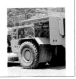

Educational and Cultural Institutions

The college catalog or prospectus is a capability brochure for an institution of higher learning. It serves both to attract potential students and to shape an image for an entity that sells not just an education but a way of life. Student/faculty interaction, facilities, and location are among the images that need be stressed. Promotional materials done in-house for Collin County Community College utilize the four *C*'s in its name to stress the "community" aspect of four separate campuses united into one system. A prospectus created by Genovese Coustenis Design for Macalester College in St. Paul, Minnesota, starts with its setting—a maple tree-covered campus—and derives a theme of "Ivy, Not Ivy," symbolized by a maple leaf, to make the point that Macalester offers an Ivy League–quality education in a different, but equally appealing, location.

Art and design school catalogs need to emphasize location to a lesser extent. The spectacular Alpine site of Art Center College of Design (Europe) is an exception—the Swiss setting is a main feature of its catalog, shown here. For art schools, facilities tend to be more important, and in-action shots of students at work are key. An image of a paint-splattered student in front of an easel is far more engaging than the same student shown in conversation with a professor. Nesnadny+Schwartz's catalog for the Cleveland Institute of Art, for example, opens with duotones that emphasize the hands-on aspect of an art education. (Depicting the art and design school experience may get more difficult, however, as computers continue to make inroads into art and design—a picture of a student at her computer is rela-tively static.) Art and design programs also provide a highly visual end product that usually needs to be featured in recruitment materials—student and alumni work. The Reed and Steven Advertising staff who worked on the Art Institute of Fort Lauderdale catalog are all alumni of that institution, and the catalog is liberally illustrated with work of students and fellow graduates, such as the Elvis postage stamp by Mark Stutzman. A brochure for Virginia Commonwealth University's newly-founded Ad Center takes the student-at-work motif to the extreme with a piece in the form of an ad assignment, leading the reader from the initial job description letter through the completed advertisement—for the Ad Center.

Exhibition and symposia catalogs for educational and cultural institutions function as documents of—and supplements to—specific events. In many cases, as in a booklet for the Allentown Art Museum's "Restraint & Surrender," the photographs on exhibition are accompanied by a curator's essay, but mainly are allowed to speak for themselves. For Phillip Unetic of 3r1 Group, this provided an opportunity to work closely with a museum professional whose achievements he greatly admires. In other cases, such as a catalog for "California: In Three Dimensions," a sculpture exhibition at the California Center for the Arts Museum, the designer's task was to incorporate artists' statements with two-dimensional images of three-dimensional works. Mires Design used the opportunity to make the catalog itself into a dimensional experience, varying concave and convex embossing and paper textures.

Designing the art school catalog can be both liberating (clients who understand creativity!) and limiting (how to incorporate all that student work?). Catalogs for The Art Institute of Fort Lauderdale and Cleveland Institute of Art approach the art-school experience from the perspective of turning an art degree into a professional career, but from divergent angles. Reed and Steven Advertising's book for the Fort Lauderdale school (this spread) seeks to lure the "MTV generation" with high-impact graphics that help answer the question, "You Mean I Can Make a Living Doing This?" The Nesnadny+Schwartz–designed book for the Cleveland institution, in contrast, stresses that CIA is a "professional college of art and design" with a more subdued yet stylish tone (p. 68). The catalog for Art Center College of Design (Europe) also presents a sophisticated look to attract older students from outside the U.S. (p. 69).

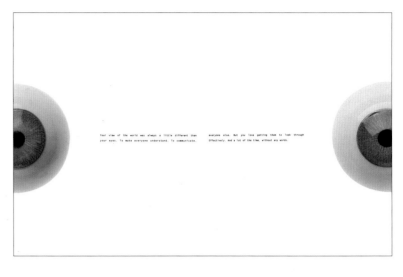

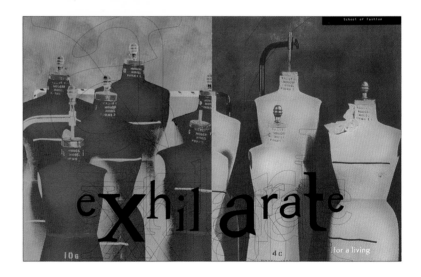

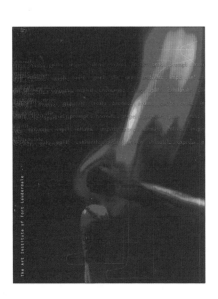

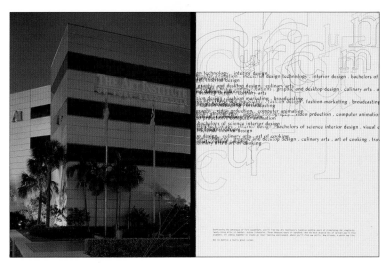

Agency:
Reed and Steven
Advertising,
Fort Lauderdale, Florida
Creative Director/
Art Director:
Joe Schovitz
Designers:
Andre Seibel, Siobhan
Elms, Matt Cave
Photographer:
Thompson & Thompson

To reach an audience of potential students from the "MTV generation," The Art Institute of Fort Lauderdale gave Reed and Steven Advertising free rein in creating this 1996–1997 catalog. The overall message, "You Mean I Can Make a Living Doing This?," is reinforced through the use of large numbers of student and alumni work—and the fact that the Reed and Steven staff members who put together the catalog are all Art Institute of Fort Lauderdale alumni. The bulk of the images were shot by Thompson & Thompson Photography (an alumnus and an instructor), with the rest taken from stock CD's. To help keep the attention of a young audience, the 8 $^1/_4$" x 10 $^3/_4$" catalog is divided into two sections: an exciting, image-filled first half, which explains the different schools and majors; and a text-only second half, which communicates more mundane curriculum and policy information. Spreads introducing sections devoted to schools within the institute (Design, Culinary and Hospitality, Fashion, etc.) employ large-scale text (done in Illustrator and sometimes imported into Photoshop) over color-saturated photographic images created in Photoshop.

THE ART INSTITUTE OF FORT LAUDERDALE

In order to conserve money and materials for the Cleveland Institute of Art's recruiting literature, Nesnadny+Schwartz conceived this catalog without any "dated" information. Course descriptions, schedules, and so forth are contained in a simple two-color addendum that is updated annually—resulting in an overall savings in creative and production budgets of approximately 50 per cent. Because the Institute's "fundamental mission" is "to provide a quality education for men and women who seek professional art careers," the catalog is stylish yet serious, focusing on "duotones" of students at work and a limited number of their creations. (The simulated "duotones" were created from black-and-white originals, scanned into a DS system as a 4-color process.) The Institute also prides itself on a state-of-the art facility, seen here in images such as one that shows students drawing from the nude model—directly on the computer. Text pages feature generous areas of white space and widely set, creatively colored and sized pieces of type. The catalog measures 8 3/4" x 13".

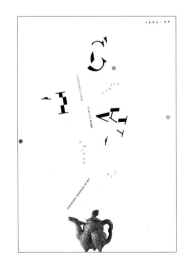

Design Firm:
Nesnadny+Schwartz,
Cleveland, Ohio
Art Directors:
Mark Schwartz,
Joyce Nesnadny
Designers:
Joyce Nesnadny,
Brian Lavy
Photographers:
Mark Schwartz,
Robert A. Muller
Copywriter:
Anne Brooks Ranallo
Printer:
Fortran Printing, Inc.

The catalog for Art Center College of Design (Europe), located in La Tour-de-Peilz, Switzerland, aims for a different audience—Europeans aged 18 to 23—than the American high-schoolers targeted by Art Center (USA). This 10" x 7 1/8" piece, while designed to be in the same family as the American catalog, reflects a more sophisticated look to attract an older, European student. The designer and photographer traveled to the Swiss campus to create the principal photography, including stunning black-and-white images of the Alpine area and color video-grabs of the students and setting. Student work is represented in both color and black-and-white. Type is stretched, distorted, and overprinted; lines are bent and pulled; and margins ebb and flow unpredictably. The fonts used range from Franklin Gothic and Helvetica to Ammama Inline, Fascinate, and Modderig. The "general information contents" of the catalog, comprising the second half of the book, are printed without images on a brown paper.

ART CENTER COLLEGE OF DESIGN (EUROPE)

Design Firm:
Art Center Design Office,
Pasadena, California
**Vice President,
Creative Director:**
Stuart I. Frolick
Design Director:
Rebeca Mendez
**Art Director/
Videographer:**
Darin Beaman
Designers:
Darin Beaman,
Chris Haaga

Associate Designer:
Susanne Holthuizen
Photographer:
Steven A. Heller
Editor:
Julie Suhr
Production Manager:
Ellie Eisner
Production Artist:
Ben Takahashi

Design Firm:
O'Keefe Marketing,
Richmond, Virginia
Creative Director:
Kelly O'Keefe
Art Director/Designer:
Jeff Schaich
Photographers:
Jon Hood, Sonny Bowyer,
Double Image Studio
Copywriter:
Tracy Tierney
Production:
Daisey Sanders

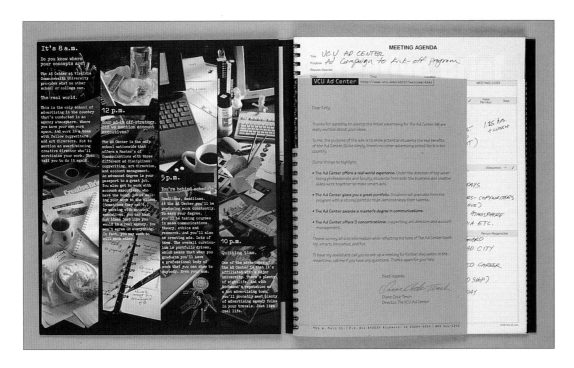

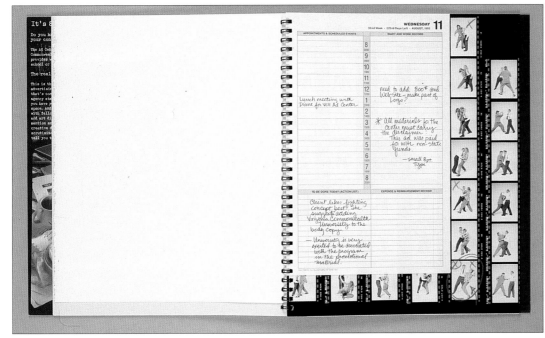

The Virginia Commonwealth University Ad Center, a new school offering Master's degrees in art direction, copywriting, and account management, is the first school to bring creatives and account executives together in a "real world" advertising agency environment. O'Keefe Marketing produced this amusing recruiting brochure pro-bono (it measures 9" x 11"). The opening spread challenges, "It's 8 A.M. Do you know where your concepts are?," and takes the reader through to quitting time (10 P.M.) with columns of text and images of working tools—and meals eaten on the run. The brochure itself then imitates the process of putting together an ad—for the Ad Center, of course—from the points of view of the three disciplines offered at the school. Fifteen pages are printed on 15 stocks (of many different sizes), including a letter on Ad Center stationery giving the assignment, a meeting agenda page with notes on the project, a napkin sketch, a page of contact prints, a blueline, and finally, the completed ad, which depicts a tie-and-suspender-wearing account exec in combat with a long-haired, Birkenstock-shod creative.

ARTHUR ANDERSEN & COMPANY

To promote Arthur Andersen & Company's Center for Professional Education, Communication Design Center created this "Stay Centered" brochure. With the aim to set the Center apart from other training centers and hotel chains, the designers commissioned well-known illustrators like Linda Bleck and Gary Kelley to produce images relating to six areas of expertise and differentiation. These full-color conceptual illustrations (balanced on each spread by small, square documentary duotones and testimonial quotes) proved so popular that they were purchased by Andersen and now hang in prominent locations at the Center, in Chicago. Because the Center recycles everything from paper to coffee grounds, recycled paper was the only appropriate choice. The entire brochure (measuring 8 1/4" x 12 1/4") is printed on Simpson Coronado SST, with a two-color engraved front cover and a gatefold back cover to accommodate specific meeting facility information and a location map for site visits.

tailored technical expertise means you can FOCUS on training

explore the CONVERGENCE of business with pleasure

education MEETS nature in our tranquil st. charles setting

stayCENTERED

Design Firm:
Communication Design Center, Munster, Indiana
Art Director:
Sue Miskovich
Designer:
Amy Charlson
Illustrators:
Ferruccio Sardella, David Lesh, Tatjana Krizmanic, Linda Bleck, Michael Dinges, Gary Kelley

Design Firm:
CCCC Publications,
Plano, Texas
Art Director/Designer:
Mark Steele

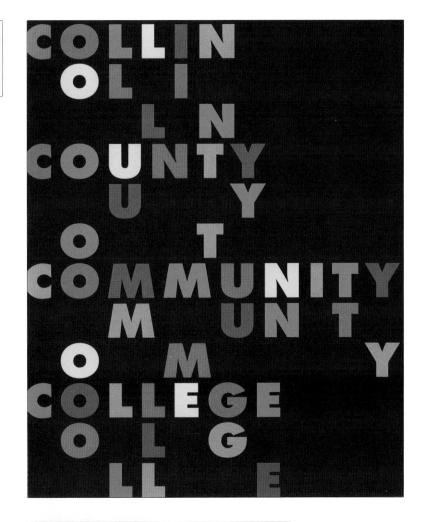

With four *C*'s and four campuses in Collin County Community College (in McKinney, Plano, and Frisco, Texas), the CCCC Publications department chose to build an identity featuring the letter *C*, black backgrounds, and bright color accents. A 6" x 9" viewpiece was created that not only supports an image of the district as a whole, but further defines the strengths of each individual campus. The viewpiece text is arranged around concepts beginning with *C*: "collaborative efforts," "career enhancement," and so forth. An 8 1/2" x 11" student handbook cover employs a motif of four *C*'s within a *C*, while the course catalog (of the same size) employs a lively color-on-black scheme to entice the reader. These materials were put together with the services of a part-time art director, full-time staff designer, freelance production, and student photography.

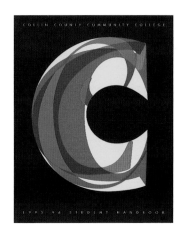

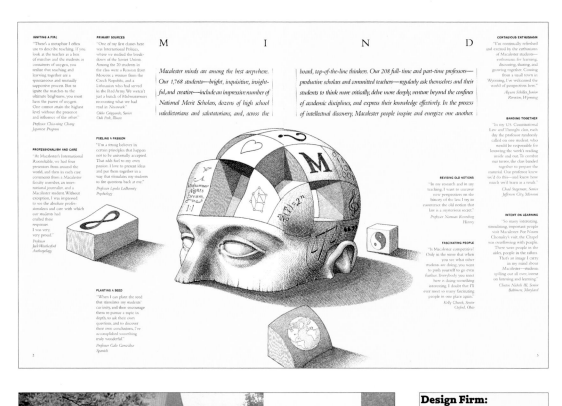

MIND

IGNITING A FIRE
"There's a metaphor I often use to describe teaching. If you look at the teacher as a box of matches and the students as containers of oxygen, you realize that teaching and learning together are a spontaneous and mutually supportive process. But to ignite the matches to the ultimate brightness, you must have the purest of oxygen. One cannot attain the highest level without the presence and influence of the other."
Professor Chia-ning Chang
Japanese Program

PROFESSIONALISM AND CARE
"At Macalester's International Roundtable, we had four presenters from around the world, and then in each case comments from a Macalester faculty member, an international journalist, and a Macalester student. Without exception, I was impressed to see the absolute professionalism and care with which our students had crafted their responses. I was very, very proud."
Professor Jack Weatherford
Anthropology

PRIMARY SOURCES
"One of my first classes here was International Politics, where we studied the breakdown of the Soviet Union. Among the 20 students in the class were a Russian from Moscow, a woman from the Czech Republic, and a Lithuanian who had served in the Red Army. We weren't just a bunch of Midwesterners recounting what we had read in *Newsweek*."
Okko Grippando, Senior
Oak Park, Illinois

FUELING A PASSION
"I'm a strong believer in certain principles that happen not to be universally accepted. That adds fuel to my own passion. I love to present ideas and put them together in a way that stimulates my students to fire questions back at me."
Professor Lynda LaBounty
Psychology

PLANTING A SEED
"When I can plant the seed that stimulates my students' curiosity, and then encourage them to pursue a topic in depth, to ask their own questions, and to discover their own conclusions, I've accomplished something truly wonderful."
Professor Galo González
Spanish

Macalester minds are among the best anywhere. Our 1,768 students—bright, inquisitive, insightful, and creative—include an impressive number of National Merit Scholars, dozens of high school valedictorians and salutatorians, and, across the board, top-of-the-line thinkers. Our 208 full-time and part-time professors—productive scholars and committed teachers—regularly ask themselves and their students to think more critically, delve more deeply, venture beyond the confines of academic disciplines, and express their knowledge effectively. In the process of intellectual discovery, Macalester people inspire and energize one another.

REVISING OLD NOTIONS
"In my research and in my teaching, I want to uncover new perspectives on the history of the law. I try to reconstruct the old notion that law is a mysterious secret."
Professor Norman Rosenberg
History

FASCINATING PEOPLE
"Is Macalester competitive? Only in the sense that when you see what other students are doing, you want to push yourself to go even further. Everybody you meet here is doing something interesting. I doubt that I'll ever meet so many fascinating people in one place again."
Kelly Church, Senior
Oxford, Ohio

CONTAGIOUS ENTHUSIASM
"I'm continually refreshed and excited by the enthusiasm of Macalester students—enthusiasm for learning, discussing, sharing, and growing together. Coming from a small town in Wyoming, I've welcomed the world of perspectives here."
Alyson Schiller, Junior
Riverton, Wyoming

BANDING TOGETHER
"In my U.S. Constitutional Law and Thought class, each day the professor randomly called on one student, who would be responsible for knowing the week's reading inside and out. To combat our terror, the class banded together to prepare the material. Our professor knew we'd do this—and knew how much we'd learn as a result."
Chad Stegman, Senior
Jefferson City, Missouri

INTENT ON LEARNING
"So many interesting, stimulating, important people visit Macalester. For Noam Chomsky's visit, the Chapel was overflowing with people. There were people in the aisles, people in the rafters. That's an image I carry in my mind about Macalester—students spilling out all over, intent on listening and learning."
Clinton Nichols III, Senior
Baltimore, Maryland

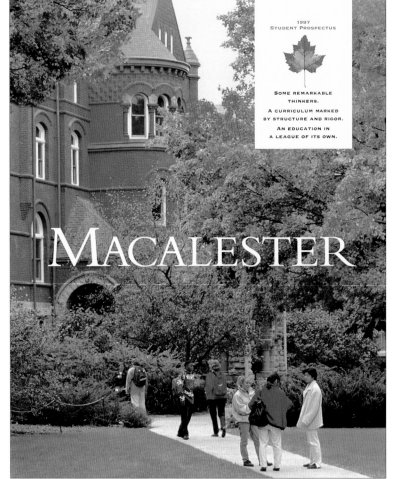

1997
STUDENT PROSPECTUS

SOME REMARKABLE THINKERS.

A CURRICULUM MARKED BY STRUCTURE AND RIGOR.

AN EDUCATION IN A LEAGUE OF ITS OWN.

MACALESTER

Design Firm:
Genovese Coustenis Design, Baltimore, Maryland
Art Director/Designer:
Domenica Genovese
Illustrator:
Laszlo Kubinyi

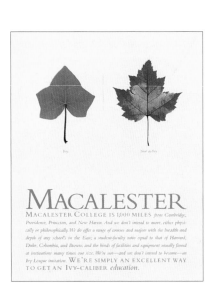

Ivy.   Not so Ivy.

MACALESTER

MACALESTER COLLEGE IS 1,000 MILES from Cambridge, Providence, Princeton, and New Haven. And we don't intend to move, either physically or philosophically. We offer a range of courses and majors with the breadth and depth of any school's in the East; a student-faculty ratio equal to that of Harvard, Duke, Columbia, and Brown; and the kinds of facilities and equipment usually found at institutions many times our size. We're not—and we don't intend to become—an Ivy League imitation. WE'RE SIMPLY AN EXCELLENT WAY TO GET AN IVY-CALIBER *education*.

ATHLETE, SCHOLAR, AND MORE

On the gridiron, Tony Micheli wears jersey 13 for the Macalester Scots, but that's the closest he comes to being a "number." In fact, precisely because he wanted to know—and be known to—other students and professors, Tony looked for a relatively small college with a strong academic reputation. He also wanted to play football and to study in an urban location. A middle linebacker and a biology major, Tony comments on the collaborative spirit at Macalester: "In athletics, we play in a very competitive conference—NCAA Division III in the Minnesota

Intercollegiate Athletic Conference. But in the classroom, even though there are a lot of pre-med majors in biology, students help each other out and don't hide information." Beyond that, he says: "I've met all kinds of people I wouldn't have met in Alpine, Texas. I have experienced 'culture shock,' but in a good way. I've kept my beliefs in place, and I accept people for what they are." Tony is looking forward to an internship with the team's orthopedic surgeon or with a Minneapolis-based physical therapist. After Macalester, he plans to earn a master's degree in physical therapy.

Anthony Micheli
Junior
Alpine, Texas
Biology major

Professor Diane Glancy
English

THE CONVERSATION OF WRITING

"Writing is a conversation," observes Diane Glancy, whose poetry, plays, essays, and fiction have earned her numerous literary prizes, including the American Book Award, the Minnesota Book Award for Poetry, and the Native-American Prose Award. "My students and I come together to take risks and reach new frontiers." For Glancy, writing has also been a journey. As artist in residence of the Oklahoma State Arts Council, she traveled the state for a decade, teaching the skills of writing, oral communication, and critical thinking to Native-American high school and college students. Her growing reputation as a writer opened

the door to a fellowship at the prestigious University of Iowa Writers' Workshop, then to a faculty position at Macalester. Glancy teaches Native-American Literature and Creative Writing, among other courses, while adding to her own body of work. Her latest novel, *Pushing the Bear*, recounts the 19th-century Cherokee "Trail of Tears" experience. "Native-American literature can be frustrating," Glancy notes. "There are many narrators and no chronological order, so you can get lost very easily. Even when it's not always comfortable, I have found Macalester students willing to stick with it. I admire their willingness to struggle and their sense of adventure. That's education."

CULTURE, SCIENCE, ADVENTURE

"I'm definitely not a one-track-mind person," observes Bridget Anderson. "I need culture, humor, science, athletics—and adventure." While at Macalester, she has lived in the German House, played bass trombone with the Jazz Band, gone on an extended field trip to the southwestern U.S., run sprints with the track team, and studied and worked in Africa. To deepen her understanding of environmental ethics, Bridget connected with a program in ecology and wildlife conservation in Tanzania. As part of that experience, she conducted independent work in Zanzibar, setting up a moni-

toring system to determine the effects of sewage pollution on the Coral Reef. After that, Bridget landed a summer job at the Jane Goodall Institute. Her summer job, working with five orphaned chimps, taught her an important lesson and pointed her to a possible career: "I learned patience, working with rambunctious chimps and trying to communicate in broken Swahili with the Tanzanians. I also learned that there is life after college. It made me excited to move on to other things." For Bridget, those "other things" include gaining more experience in ecology and education (possibly working at a zoo), and then heading to graduate school.

Bridget Anderson
Senior
Duluth, Minnesota
Geology major
Biology/German minors

Professor J. Andrew Overman
Classics

REINVENTING THE CLASSICS

When Andy Overman notes the recent upsurge in classics majors at Macalester—from 6 in 1993 to about 24 today—one cannot help but conclude that his unbridled enthusiasm for the discipline is a contributing factor, along with his eagerness to involve students in research and his ability to draw parallels between current social issues and ancient civilizations. "As a department, we take students into the world," he says. "We put flesh on internationalism." Overman had only been here a few months in 1993 when he started laying the groundwork for an archaeological dig in the former Soviet Union. In summer 1994, the Macalester Black Sea Project was

launched outside Sevastopol on Ukraine's Crimean Peninsula. Joining Overman were 12 Macalester students and 17 students and scholars from Ukraine's Zaporozhye University, a project co-sponsor. The excavations of a first-century synagogue and other sites are focusing on the multicultural nature of the ancient city of Chersonesus during the Greco-Roman period. "This ancient city," Overman comments, "was a successful experiment in democracy for well over a millennium, and can help us understand questions of ethnicity in our own world." The work in Zaporozhye continues. In addition, the department sponsors a program in Rome and is preparing another in Jerusalem.

To attract highly motivated students to Macalester College, Genovese Coustenis Design developed this 8 ½" x 11" prospectus around the themes of "Mind" and "Moment," distilled from the school's belief that hard work and disciplined inquiry can lead to moments of unusual insight. Laszlo Kubinyi was commissioned to illustrate these concepts—and add a touch of humor—for the brochure's first two spreads. While the institution wanted a full-bleed photo showing the campus and students for the prospectus cover, a drawing of a maple leaf inset in a box at upper right adds a third theme of "Ivy, not Ivy" to suggest that the Saint Paul, Minnesota, school offers an Ivy League–quality education in a Midwestern setting.

MACALESTER COLLEGE

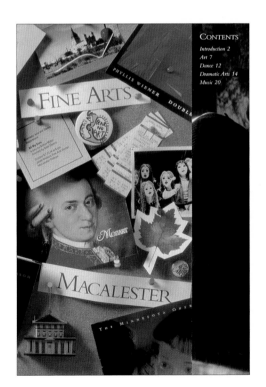

FINE ARTS

MACALESTER

CONTENTS

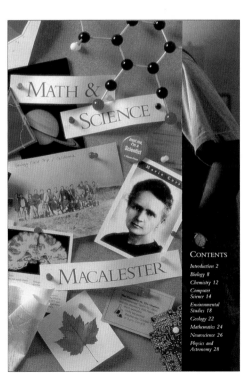

MATH & SCIENCE

MACALESTER

CONTENTS

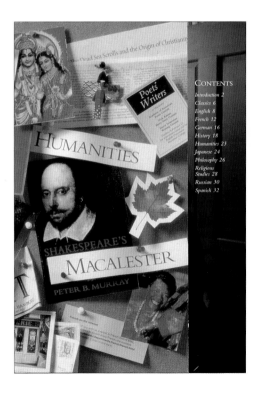

HUMANITIES

MACALESTER

CONTENTS

All three college promotions shown here share a fine-art sensibility. A direct-mail brochure for the University of Iowa Hospitals and Clinics Department of Ophthalmology (p. 79) takes its visual motif from a painting titled "Chairs," to raise money to "endow" chairs in the school's auditorium. A brochure for the UCLA Theater Department, created by Kimberly Baer Design Associates and illustrated with original monoprint etchings by Maria Horusiewicz (p. 78), serves not only as a form for ticket orders by mail, but also to attract funding organizations and students. A Visual Asylum–designed piece commissioned by the University of San Diego to honor its art-loving president upon his retirement (this spread) is a fine-art object in itself: Only eight copies of this letterpress and lithograph color plate illustrated book were printed.

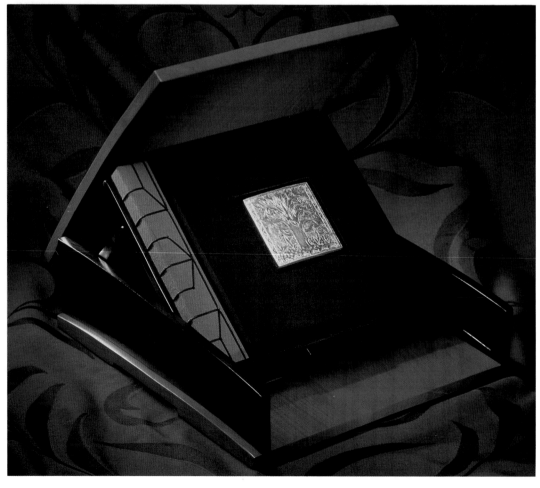

Design Firm:
Visual Asylum,
San Diego, California
Art Directors:
MaeLin Levine, Amy Jo
Levine
Designers:
Jason Janus, MaeLin
Levine, Amy Jo Levine
Illustrators/Painters/
Photographers:
Norman Walker, David
Diaz, Clem Bedwell, Joel
Peter Johnson, Fred
Otnes, Troy Viss, Philipp
Scholz Rittermann

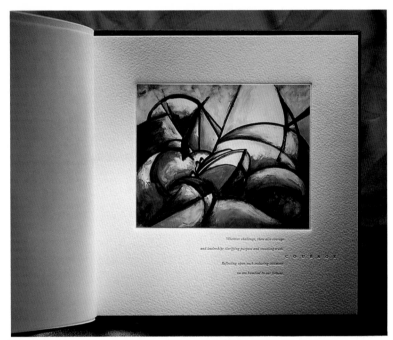

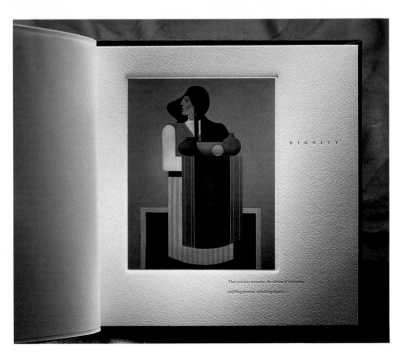

The University Relations Division commissioned this limited-edition book to honor Dr. Author E. Hughes, retiring president of the University of San Diego, after 20 years of service. Visual Asylum was asked to incorporate Dr. Hughes's diverse interests—from sailing to Native American art—into this special gift, which combines letterpress and litho color plates illustrated with a mix of stock, fine art, and commissioned images. Each page treats a special quality, such as "courage," "dignity," and "understanding." Only eight books were printed—one for the president and seven for the artists involved. They are hand-bound in a Japanese style and stored in a specially designed case that forms a shelf when opened for ease in viewing.

THE UNIVERSITY OF SAN DIEGO

The UCLA Theater Department turned to Kimberly Baer Design Associates for this direct-mail brochure, which needed not only to satisfy current subscribers and attract new ticket buyers, but also impress funding organizations, industry partners, and potential students. The 8" x 8 1/2" brochure had to be produced on a tight budget and mail easily and inexpensively. Baer commissioned original monoprint etchings from fine artist/illustrator Maria Horusiewicz to represent each of the plays offered, ranging from Garcia Lorca's *Blood Wedding* to *The Illusion,* Tony Kushner's adaptation of Corneille's classic comedy.

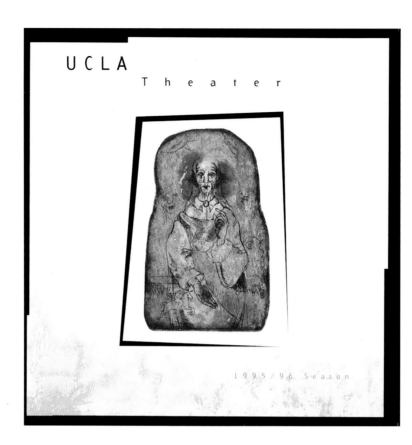

Design Firm:
Kimberly Baer Design Associates, Venice, California
Art Director:
Kimberly Baer
Designer:
Barbara Cooper
Illustrator:
Maria Horusiewicz

Design Firm:
University of Iowa
Foundation,
Iowa City, Iowa
Art Director/Designer:
Richard Blazek
Artist:
Byron L. Burford
Copywriter:
Susan Shullaw

ONE HUNDRED TEN

CHAIRS

THE "110 CHAIRS IN OPHTHALMOLOGY" CAMPAIGN

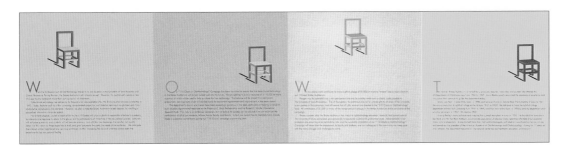

This 8 1/2" x 8 1/2" direct-mail fundraising brochure for the University of Iowa Hospitals and Clinics Department of Ophthalmology had to be produced quickly and economically by the University of Iowa Foundation. The department head requested that a favorite painting by an emeritus art and art history professor be used. The painting—"Chairs," by Byron L. Burford—eliminated the need for expensive photography or illustration, and provided an appropriate image for the "110 Chairs in Ophthalmology" campaign, to "endow" chairs in the 110-seat Braley Auditorium. The designer traced an outline of a chair from the painting and repeated it, guided by the painting's palette, on the Productolith dull-coated text panels of the brochure. The picture is also reproduced in black-and-white (with a strip of pink) on the brochure's white mailing envelope. The playful colors and simple geometric shapes derived from the painting achieve an exuberance and enthusiasm not often found in medical fundraising materials.

The design of exhibition and symposium catalogs must generally take place within two difficult-to-reconcile parameters: a need to satisfy a visually sophisticated audience, and an extremely limited budget. The four catalogs shown here are divided between two color strategies that aid them in achieving results within these requirements: black-and-white with punchy additions of red, or shades of bright yellow set off with glossy blacks. A catalog produced by Mires Design for the California Center for the Arts Museum's "California: In Three Dimensions" sculpture show (this spread) alternates yellow text pages printed with heavy black type with photos of artworks on glossy stock. The folder holding press and curriculum materials by Grafik Communications Ltd. for the Smithsonian Institution's "Earth 2U, Exploring Geography" exhibition (pp. 82–83) utilizes angular die-cuts to create interest, along with Marc Rosenthal's cartoony illustrations. Yellow is also the main color. In contrast, Phillip Unetic of 3r1 Group and Sanft Design employ mainly black-and-white palettes for their catalogs. Unetic's book for the Allentown Art Museum (p. 85) relies on red to add to the emotional tone of the photographs in "Restraint & Surrender." Sanft uses red to add contrast to photos and drawings of works by Frank Lloyd Wright in two volumes for Arizona State University (p. 86).

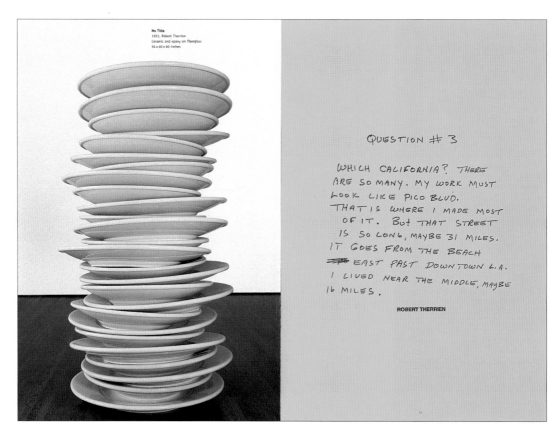

No Title
1993, Robert Therrien
Ceramic and epoxy on fiberglass
94 x 60 x 60 inches

QUESTION # 3

WHICH CALIFORNIA? THERE
ARE SO MANY. MY WORK MUST
LOOK LIKE PICO BLVD.
THAT IS WHERE I MADE MOST
OF IT. But THAT STREET
IS SO LONG, MAYBE 31 MILES.
IT GOES FROM THE BEACH
EAST PAST DOWNTOWN L.A.
I LIVED NEAR THE MIDDLE, MAYBE
16 MILES.

ROBERT THERRIEN

California: In
Three Dimensions
May 21 through August 25, 1995
Opening Party
May 20, 1995. 6:00–8:00 p.m.
Members free, non-members $4.
Live music by the Swingin' Kings,
dancing and refreshments.

Peter Shelton Lecture
May 20, 5:00 p.m. Free admission.
Artists
Peter Shelton, Robert Therrien,
Peter Walker, Mary Bates, Rob
Craigie, Tom Driscoll, Mineko
Grimmer, Tim Hawkinson, Tina
Hulett, Jay Johnson, Mark Lere,
Anne Mudge, Tomas Nakada,
Minoru Ohira, Ross Rudel, Melissa
Smedley, and Daniel Wheeler.

**California Center for
the Arts Museum**
340 North Escondido Boulevard
Escondido, California 92025
619-738-4120

California: In Three Dimensions
explores the connections and
boundaries between painting
and sculpture, in both abstract
and semi-abstract work of contemporary California artists.

california: In Three Dimensions

Design Firm:
Mires Design, Inc.,
San Diego, California
Art Director/Designer:
John Ball

On view at the California Center for the Arts Museum in 1995 was "California: In Three Dimensions," an exhibition of "painterly-sculpture" or "fat painting." Mires Design's distinctive bright yellow catalog takes its visual cues both from "the reflected light that fills the air in California" and the concern with surface and texture evident in the works on view. The exhibition title is embossed on the 8" x 12" catalog's cover, alternating convex and concave letters, and the book is packaged in a die-cut slipcase. Artists' essays are printed on paper of the same yellow color inside the book; these pages are folded because the heavier yellow stock used for the cover was unavailable. The yellow sheets alternate with coated pages featuring photographs of the exhibited art works. Most of the photos were provided by the artists, and shadows and white backgrounds were added to some in Photoshop. The catalog design was carried through on invitations, postcards, and a newspaper ad.

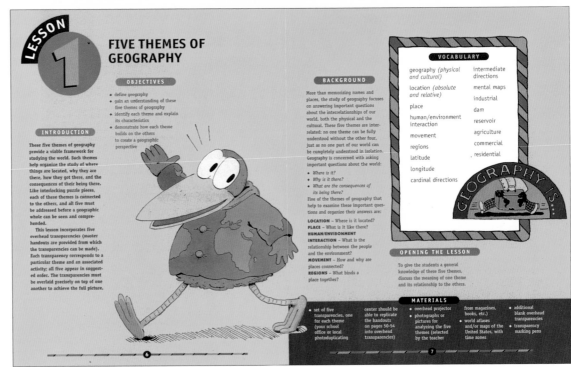

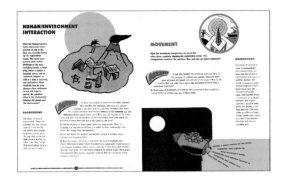

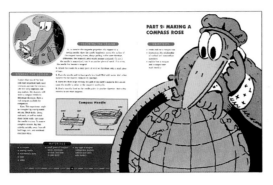

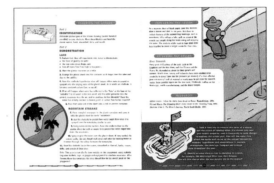

The exhibition "Earth 2U, Exploring Geography," organized by the Smithsonian Institution Traveling Exhibition Service (SITES) and the National Geographic Society, is traveling to museums across the country through the year 2002. Grafik Communications Ltd. prepared this 10" x 13 1/2" (irregular) folder, press kit, and curriculum guide to assist in encouraging children to explore the world around them. Illustrations by Marc Rosenthal are employed both in the exhibition and its accompanying materials. The curriculum guide highlights the exhibition mascot, a bird named "Seymour D. Earth." The main text and folder colors derive from Seymour's beak. To reflect the illustrator's angular use of shadows and to give the presentation an unusual twist, the folder was die-cut with angled edges and pockets. The curriculum guide, which includes maps, charts, and other handouts to be duplicated for classroom use, is as fun to read for adults as the activities are designed to be for kids. And, as for organization of materials, the introduction assures teachers, "You won't need a map to navigate the curriculum guide!"

Design Firm:
Grafik Communications, Ltd., Alexandria, Virginia
Designers:
David Collins, Richard Hamilton, Judy Kirpich
Illustrator:
Marc Rosenthal

Restraint & Surrender

PHOTOGRAPHS BY KEN GRAVES AND EVA LIPMAN

Design Firm:
3r1 Group, Willow Grove,
Pennsylvania
Art Director/Designer:
Phillip Unetic
Photographers:
Ken Graves, Eva Lipman

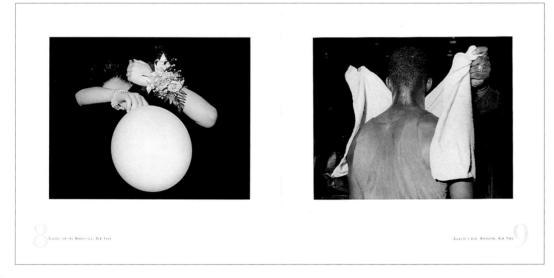

The catalog for "Restraint & Surrender" documents a 1995 Allentown Art Museum exhibition of the unusual collaborative photographs of Ken Graves and Eva Lipman. High reproduction quality on a low museum budget was the main design requirement, and all photographs were reproduced at least as duotones and 350-line screens. In his design, Phillip Unetic of 3r1 Group wanted to maintain the emotional impact of seeing the photographs for the first time. The large page format (11" x 10 3/4") allows for high impact and made large blow-ups on the inside covers possible. While most of the catalog is printed in black, white, and gray, a judicious use of red—for the ampersand in the title on the cover and title page, and as an overlay on the inside cover photos—heightens the emotional tone of the layout, in keeping with the mood of the photographs. Only 2500 copies of the catalog were printed, by a print shop that specializes in small-run art publications.

The two volumes of *Frank Lloyd Wright: The Phoenix Papers* reproduce material from two symposia exploring Wright's contribution to American design, held in 1991 at the Herberger Center for Design Excellence, College of Architecture and Environmental Design, Arizona State University. Sanft Design was hired to create books that would communicate Wright's philosophy in visual form, would stand out on a coffee table, and could be produced at a low cost. *Volume I* treats Wright's design for Broadacre City, which was based on a square further divided into four one-mile squares. This concept of divided squares became the basis for Sanft's design: The book, when opened, is square; the text is printed in square blocks; and some text blocks are further divided into four squares, with quotes rotated randomly among them. *Volume II: The Natural Patterns of Structure*, likewise builds upon Wright's designs. Each book measures 7" x 14". Both softcover and hardcover versions were published, with slipcased hardcover sets serving as gifts.

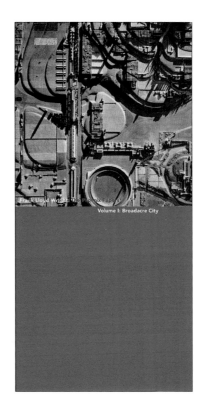

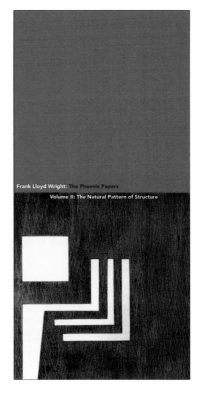

Design Firm:
Sanft Design Inc.,
Tempe, Arizona
Art Director:
Alfred Sanft

ANNUAL REPORTS

Of all the booklet and brochure types featured in this book, the designer's creativity and vision are perhaps most restricted by the annual report. As a legal document that must be filed with the Securities and Exchange Commission, the annual report designer can't get too fancy—no deconstructed financials here. But the very constrictions on these documents may cause designers to work smarter and tighter, and annual reports are often the best of the best booklets and brochures.

Top-quality illustration always works, especially when a company is trying to get across that it cares for people or provides an abstract product or service. Cahan & Associates took this route by commissioning Jeffrey Fisher to help explain what Rational Software does—and why anyone should care. Edward Walter Design, too, used an illustrator known for his warm drawing style—Jack Unruh—to create a timeline depicting the highlights of MRJ Group's information solutions. Linda Frichtel's whimsical illustrations, commissioned by Laughing Dog Creative, underscore that HealthCare COMPARE, a medical cost management firm, keeps the needs of real people and not just companies, in mind.

A strictly limited color palette and visual appearance can also be highly successful, particularly when designing for non-profits—with their limited budgets and clear social missions. Black, white, and red continue to be popular colors. But what else would you use for the American Red Cross? Lewis Advertising, however, adds a twist by diecutting a cross on the report cover, revealing a red page beneath; and by die-cutting the cross out of red stock for interior pages, to frame black-and-white photos of Red Cross workers and beneficiaries on adjoining pages. Addison Corporate Annual Reports uses simple, linear graphics composed from typographical elements like arrows, printed on black stock, to convey the streamlining that took place within the American Arbitration Association in 1994. The South Texas College of Law saw a new dean taking the helm, and the Geer Design–created report employs vellum overlays to form "before and after" illustrations to suggest stricter moral codes for those practicing law.

Annual reports need not be completely sober— particularly if created for the communications and entertainment industries. Petrick Design's book for Jacor Communications, the nation's eighth-largest radio group, takes the concept of a "sound year" for the company to a logical end, providing an overview on an audio CD. In shades of fluorescent pinks and red, the Jacor annual report is a real attention-getter. A wacky radio group report is one thing—but what about the insurance industry? Two of the handsomest—and most unusual— reports emerged from this traditionally conservative industry. Nesnadny+Schwartz has a long track record of producing innovative, artistic reports for the Progressive Corporation, and 1994's report is no exception. Silhouettes of heads by artist Carter Kustera complement a theme of "diversity" in an evocative rather than specific manner. And WYD Design proves that the reinsurance industry need not be dull with its "Not Boring" report for the Zurich Reinsurance Centre. Distorted and color-saturated images of foodstuffs like bottles of hot sauce and Jiffy Pop add punch to an otherwise poker-faced industry.

The annual reports of the two biotechnology companies featured in this section use the same approach—the scientific notebook format—to different ends. Shaman Pharmaceuticals, because it develops ethnobotanical products from plants found in tropical rainforests, asserts an environmentally-friendly image in a report designed to appear low-cost by Cahan & Associates (pp. 92–93). A green cover and photos of the forest taken by scientists provide an authentic in-the-field look. The Van Dyke Company's book for ICOS, on the other hand, presents a high-tech, in-the-lab aspect, with black-and-white photos of scientists and their equipment, and magnified images from their experiments (p. 90). Leimer Cross Design, in its annual report for Penwest (this spread), which manufactures carbohydrate-based chemicals for the pharmaceutical industry (among others), similarly employs grainy black-and-white images of employees and equipment at work. HealthCare COMPARE, a medical cost management firm, uses warm-fuzzy illustrations in a book by Laughing Dog Creative to emphasize a concern for people over the bottom line (p. 91).

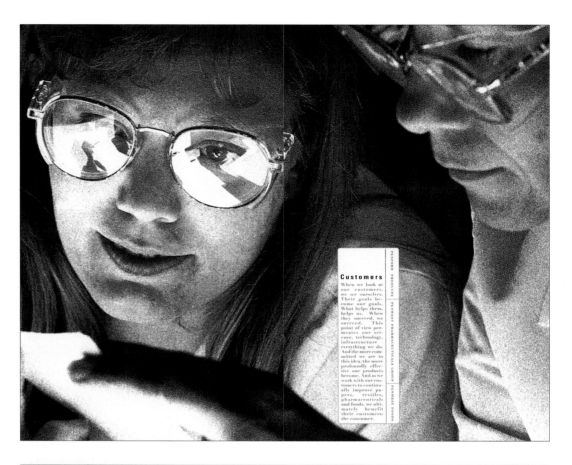

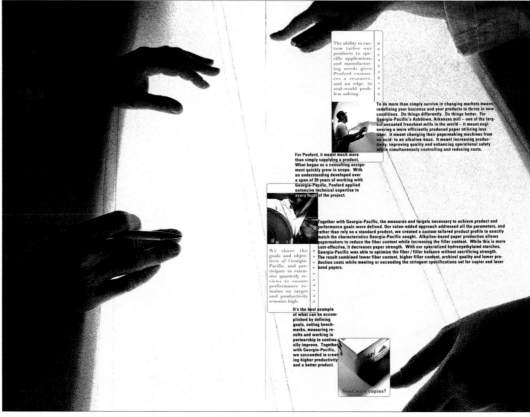

Design Firm:
Leimer Cross Design,
Seattle, Washington
Art Director/Designer:
Kerry Leimer
Photographer:
Jeff Corwin

Penwest develops, manufactures, and markets carbohydrate-based chemicals for the pharmaceutical, paper, textile, and food industries. In creating the 1995 Penwest annual report, Leimer Cross Design decided to base all photography and copy on direct client interviews. Images were reproduced as duotones from black-and-white prints, which were scanned with an unsharp mask to enhance film grain. This black-and-white photographic approach set the tone for the remaining design decisions: black and gray ink on white paper, with a touch of red type. Even the Penwest president/CEO's photograph is printed as a high key black-and-white duotone on a short page insert in his letter to shareholders. Color images appear on the inside cover, printed in small blocks on the flap of a vellum jacket. Because the report is printed on a variety of papers manufactured using Penwest products, a colophon on the back cover flap provides details about the production process, from the use of a sculptured blind emboss on the jacket and blind deboss on the cover to the fonts employed throughout (Univers 67 and Didot Bold Extended). The book measures 7" x 11".

PENWEST

ICOS CORPORATION

ICOS Corporation is a fairly new company that develops biotherapeutic medications. Because ICOS's first product moved into clinical trials in 1994, Van Dyke Company designed the annual report for that year to take the reader through the therapeutical development process, from "potential" to "discovery." Black-and-white photographs of company employees, equipment, and scientific experiments (like before-and-after treatment shots of tissue sections of a rodent trachea in an asthma model) were shot specifically for use in this report. The majority of the text is printed in gray; the only other color touches in the report come from blocks of red text, and a limited use of a gold text ink. The 8 1/2" x 11" perfect-bound book, with rounded right-hand corners, suggests a scientific notebook, and is printed on Simpson Coronado SST Recycled.

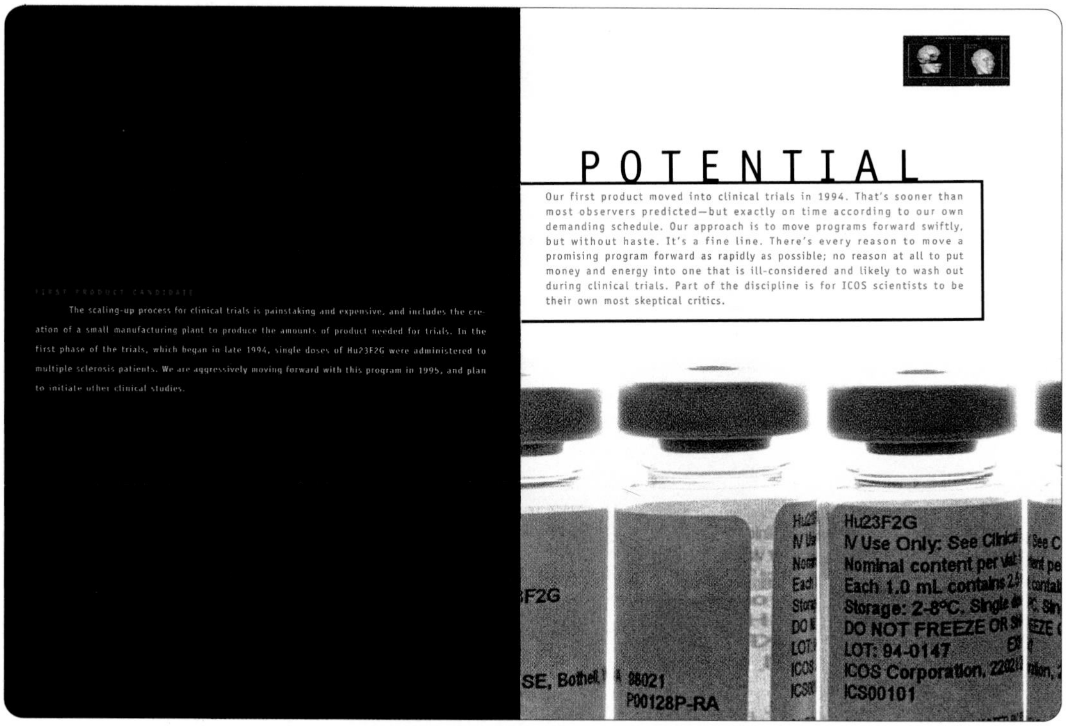
FIRST PRODUCT CANDIDATE
The scaling-up process for clinical trials is painstaking and expensive, and includes the creation of a small manufacturing plant to produce the amounts of product needed for trials. In the first phase of the trials, which began in late 1994, single doses of Hu23F2G were administered to multiple sclerosis patients. We are aggressively moving forward with this program in 1995, and plan to initiate other clinical studies.
POTENTIAL
Our first product moved into clinical trials in 1994. That's sooner than most observers predicted—but exactly on time according to our own demanding schedule. Our approach is to move programs forward swiftly, but without haste. It's a fine line. There's every reason to move a promising program forward as rapidly as possible; no reason at all to put money and energy into one that is ill-considered and likely to wash out during clinical trials. Part of the discipline is for ICOS scientists to be their own most skeptical critics.
Hu23F2G
IV Use Only
Each 1.0 mL
DO NOT FREEZE
LOT: 94-0147
ICOS Corporation
ICS00101
P00128P-RA

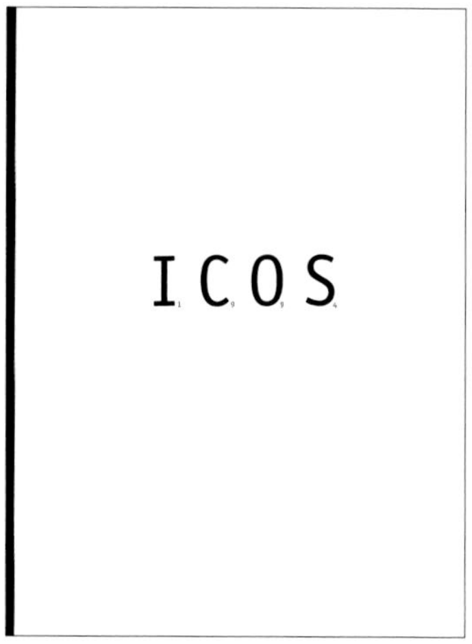
ICOS

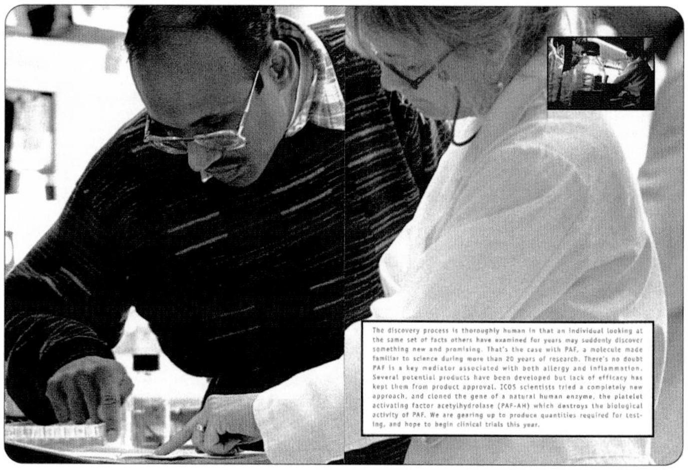
The discovery process is thoroughly human in that an individual looking at the same set of facts others have examined for years may suddenly discover something new and promising. That's the case with PAF, a molecule made familiar to science during more than 20 years of research. There's no doubt PAF is a key mediator associated with both allergy and inflammation. Several potential products have been developed but lack of efficacy has kept them from product approval. ICOS scientists tried a completely new approach, and cloned the gene of a natural human enzyme, the platelet activating factor acetylhydrolase (PAF-AH) which destroys the biological activity of PAF. We are gearing up to produce quantities required for testing, and hope to begin clinical trials this year.

Design Firm:
Van Dyke Company,
Seattle, Washington
Art Director:
John Van Dyke
Designers:
John Van Dyke,
Ann Kumasaka
Photographer:
Jeff Corwin
Copywriter:
Tom McCarthy
Printer:
MacDonald Printing

The Managed Pharmacy System not only manages prescription drug costs, it also provides a means for early intervention and case management that could save thousands of additional dollars while improving patient outcomes. • Through the online linkage of our network of retail and mail service pharmacies with our Utilization Management programs, HealthCare COMPARE Corp. electronically monitors pharmaceutical data, identifying those cases appropriate for intervention early in the treatment process. • For the first time we have the ability to identify and track patients, even before they might face the possibility of a hospital admission. When we receive information that indicates a particular case may benefit from review, our case managers then have the opportunity to recommend alternative, cost-saving treatment plans that can help the payer and patient save on both medical and pharmaceutical costs. • Additionally, our system applies more than 80 Drug Use Evaluation "edits" to each pharmaceutical transaction which enable us to review, analyze and interpret drug use information almost instantly. The system helps network providers identify problems such as too-early or too-late refills, insufficient or excessive duration of drug therapy and drug-to-drug interactions before potentially serious complications, and resulting expensive treatments, can ensue.

12

13

Expanding
the Boundaries
of Medical Cost Management

1994 Annual Report
HealthCare COMPARE Corp.

An Expanding Philosophy of Managed Care

For years HealthCare COMPARE Corp. has approached medical cost management as a function of price times volume. To generate cost savings we negotiate low prices with our providers by offering them increased numbers of patients. We then focus on volume of care through utilization management, which eliminates medically unnecessary hospitalization, facilitates delivery of needed care and identifies cost-effective treatment alternatives. • While this formula has helped us achieve outstanding success in the past, there comes a time in every industry when companies must reassess their philosophies and methodologies in order to keep pace with the changing needs of their clients. • In 1994, COMPARE began to undergo a subtle philosophical shift. It was a shift that would guide us toward more cost-efficient methods of managing quality medical care. The focus of this shift is exemplified best by our Point-of-Service program and Managed Pharmacy System. Both are aimed at achieving more tightly managed health care systems and applying a structured, integrated approach to cost control.
• Our Point-of-Service (POS) program provides unparalleled control over medical costs by

linking our referral management system with network monitoring and utilization management activities to form a comprehensive managed care program. The Managed Pharmacy System complements our POS program through additional monitoring systems which provide early identification of patients with medical conditions appropriate for intervention, chart the drug prescribing habits of our network providers and determine whether patients are using their medication appropriately. • Together these programs provide COMPARE with access to information from the moment medical care and treatment is commenced. This in turn leads to unprecedented opportunities to achieve medical care cost savings through early intervention that is followed by our on-going, supportive involvement. • Now we have taken one more step beyond the boundaries of traditional medical cost management. We have introduced a totally new concept that focuses our resources and proven techniques on all aspects of a specific disease in order to have a greater impact on the outcome of individual cases. • Cardiac care, oncological treatment and organ transplants are three areas

Client Savings

6

7

Because 1994 saw a great deal of heated debate over health care reform, the HealthCare COMPARE Corporation annual report for that year had to offer concrete evidence that the medical cost management firm would be prepared to lead the industry in 1995. Laughing Dog Creative structured the 1994 report, titled "Expanding the Boundaries of Medical Cost Management," like a children's book, with the goal of using warm-toned illustrations and accessible copy to communicate COMPARE's message for the future. The image on the opening spread shows a briefcase-toting executive looking through an eyeglass, with a triangle of yellow light issuing forth to represent his field of vision. The yellow color is carried through the next few text pages (the table of contents and president's letter), and then becomes a border around white pages featuring illustrations and text to enumerate "An Expanding Philosophy of Managed Care." The financial pages are printed on a deeper yellow stock. The book, at 7" x 10", is relatively small for an annual report.

Design Firm:
Laughing Dog Creative, Inc., Chicago, Illinois
Art Director:
Frank E.E. Grubich
Designer:
Tim Meyer
Illustrator:
Linda Frichtel

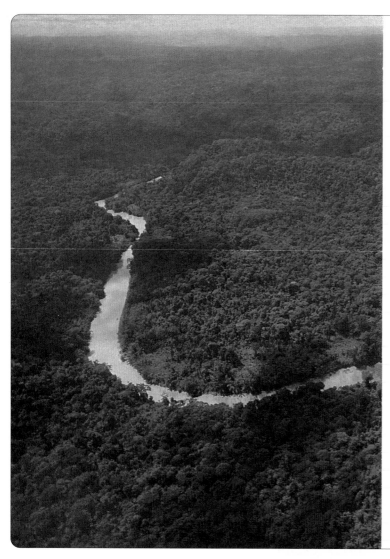

May 20, 1994
Quichua Indian village in Amazon Rainforest of Ecuador

Steven, Cesar, and I presented non-insulin dependent diabetes mellitus case presentations with signs, symptoms, and disease photographs to Elias, the village shaman. Elias stated that he recognized the disease and preceeded to describe a number of patients he had effectively treated with botanical medicines. The signs and symptoms of the patients he described included increased urination, pain and numbness of legs, infected feet sores that would not heal, and generalized weakness. He said that if the patients were not treated with the botanical medicine, they would eventually die from the disease.

Tom Carlson

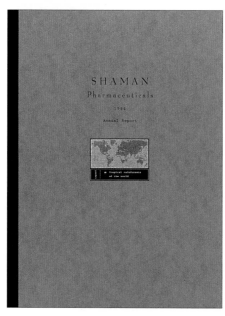

Design Firm:
Cahan & Associates,
San Francisco, California
Art Director:
Bill Cahan
Designer:
Sharrie Brooks
Photographer:
Bill McLeod

Shaman Pharmaceuticals discovers and develops pharmaceutical products by isolating active compounds from tropical plants with a history of medicinal use. While most annual report assignments involve eking an expensive appearance out of a low budget, this 1994 report, designed by Cahan & Associates, was meant to look inexpensive. In addition, the report need to bridge the mysticism of ethnobotany and the company's biotechnology foundation. Cahan & Associates chose a field log format, printing the 7 7/8" x 10 7/8" perfect-bound, die-cut radius-cornered book on uncoated stock. It opens with a facsimile of one scientist's journal entry. The imagery—from 35mm transparencies shot by Shaman scientists on a field study in the rain forest—was provided by the client and enhanced in Photoshop, with supplementary lab shots commissioned from Bill McLeod. The full-bleed photograph of the Amazon River used for the opening spread (beginning on the book's inside cover and continued on the back inside cover) was actually taken from a plane window. Because the color was quite washed out, four rounds of color proofs were needed to push the color to a maximum, and even then, the color still had to be brought up on press.

The four annual reports for non-profit organizations and institutions shown here achieve remarkably high-impact impressions considering the limited means with which they were created. The two people-oriented organizations, the Boy Scouts of America and the American Red Cross, engage the viewer with low-tech yet effective "interactive" devices. Gray Kirk Vansant Advertising's annual report for the Baltimore Area Council (this spread) asks the reader to untie a Boy Scout knot before it can even be opened. Red interior pages with die-cut crosses at the center both isolate and unite the faces of Red Cross volunteers and beneficiaries in an annual report designed for the Birmingham Area Chapter by Lewis Advertising (pp. 98–99). The reports for two legal organizations, the American Arbitration Association and the South Texas College of Law, present similarly stripped-down visions of the future for a profession that is increasingly under attack. Geer Design even uses vellum overlays in the South Texas report (pp. 100–101) to suggest a "before-and-after" effect in which less is more: When the vellum page is lifted, the underlying image is simplified—and morally repaired. Addison Corporate Annual Reports' book for the American Arbitration Association goes a step further, eliminating imagery altogether, except for small black-and-white portraits of staff members, and linear, text-based diagrams (pp. 96–97).

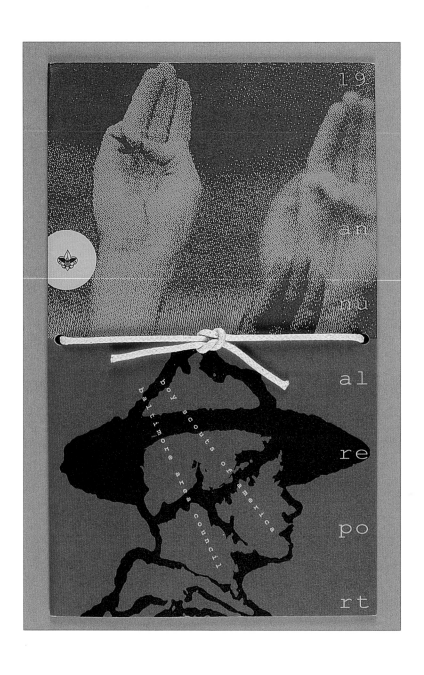

Design Firm:
Gray Kirk Vansant
Advertising, Baltimore,
Maryland
Designer:
Gene Valle
Production Manager:
Sherri Katz

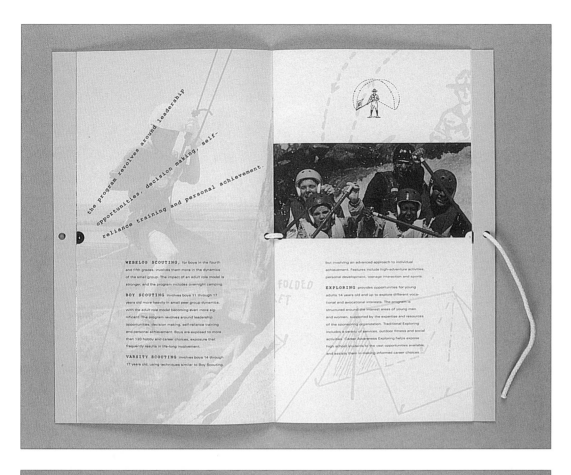

The only restriction given to Gray Kirk Vansant Advertising by the Boy Scouts of America, Baltimore Area Council, concerning this pro-bono 1994 annual report and recruitment piece was to limit the book to three colors. GKV involves the viewer from the very first by requiring him or her to untie the proverbial Boy Scout square knot that closes the cover. Archival photographs were provided by the organization, and some of the art was generated by taking supplied halftones and blowing them out on the photocopier.

Dr. Benjamin L. Harris donated line art from his collection of scouting imagery from the past century. The book is printed with soy inks on recycled paper, Benefit Ochre and Chalk, donated by Champion. Binding was done by Opportunity Builders, with the knot-tying done by mentally-challenged individuals. The 8" x 13 1/2" booklet is designed to be mailed as is, without an envelope.

BOY SCOUTS OF AMERICA, BALTIMORE AREA COUNCIL

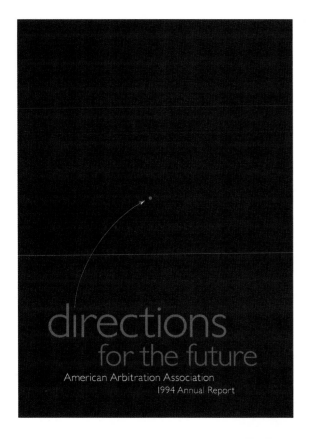

directions
for the future
American Arbitration Association
1994 Annual Report

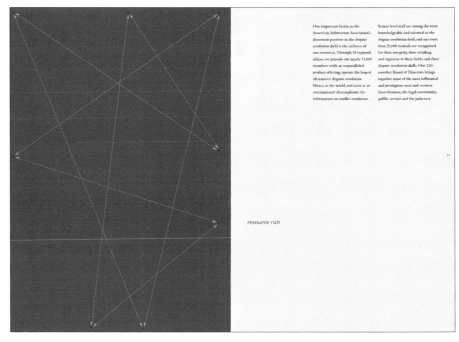

One important factor in the American Arbitration Association's dominant position in the dispute resolution field is the richness of our resources. Through 35 regional offices, we provide our nearly 13,000 members with an unparalleled product offering, operate the largest alternative dispute resolution library in the world, and serve as an international clearinghouse for information on conflict resolution.

Senior-level staff are among the most knowledgeable and talented in the dispute resolution field, and our more than 25,000 neutrals are recognized for their integrity, their standing and expertise in their fields, and their dispute resolution skills. Our 120-member Board of Directors brings together some of the most influential and prestigious men and women from business, the legal community, public service and the judiciary.

resource rich

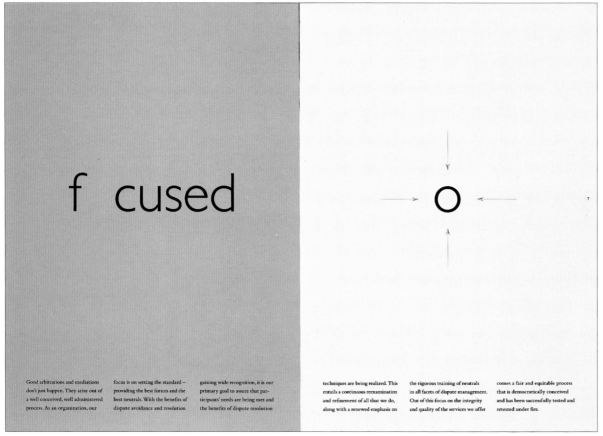

f cused

o

Good arbitrations and mediations don't just happen. They arise out of a well conceived, well administered process. As an organization, our focus is on setting the standard – providing the best forum and the best neutrals. With the benefits of dispute avoidance and resolution gaining wide recognition, it is our primary goal to assure that participants' needs are being met and the benefits of dispute resolution techniques are being realized. This entails a continuous reexamination and refinement of all that we do, along with a renewed emphasis on the rigorous training of neutrals in all facets of dispute management. Out of this focus on the integrity and quality of the services we offer comes a fair and equitable process that is democratically conceived and has been successfully tested and retested under fire.

Design Firm:
Addison Corporate,
New York, New York
Creative Director:
Victor Rivera
Art Director/Designer:
Cindy Goldstein
Printer:
Innovation

education driven

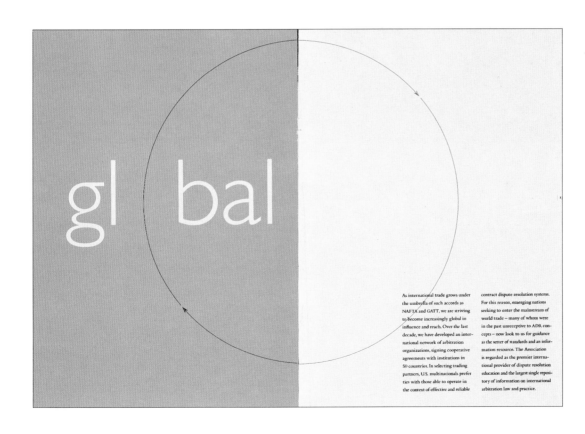

gl bal

The American Arbitration Association provides alternative dispute resolution throughout the world. Designing under budget and time limitations—and for an organization that works in abstract ideas—Addison Corporate Annual Reports developed a type-only concept for this 1994 book. Imagery is limited to black-and-white photos of officers and graphics composed in Adobe Illustrator from type and typographic elements (mainly arrows) and geometric shapes. A touch of elegant color is achieved with the use of a beige rather than white stock, and pages are printed on black, red, and olive stocks (all Mohawk Superfine) as well. The resulting document (which measures 7 3/4" x 11") austerely but attractively presents the story of a year when the AAA streamlined its operating structure, after a new senior management team took the reins.

Design Firm:
Lewis Advertising,
Birmingham, Alabama
Art Director:
Robert Froedge
Designers:
Brian Fink, Robert
Froedge
Photographers:
Mark Gooch, Randy Crow
Production:
Giannina Stephens
Copywriter:
Allen Whitley

Grover Martin knows there was a moment when he actually died on an operating table. He doesn't tell any stories of a white light or voices, but he acts every bit like a man re-born. After 30 years in the military, the retired Navy Chief had a hard time adjusting to civilian life. "All of a sudden, people who were part of your group just excluded you." He remembers. "My health was terrible. My stomach ruptured, and I had to have twenty-one pints of blood in six days. My job went out the window…I was as low as I could get." So at age 55, Grover started all over. He emerged from a VA hospital with a strong desire to use his second chance by taking care of others. His opportunity came when he entered Betty Nichols' Red Cross nursing assistant training program. He says, "Betty is just a brilliant instructor. We learned things in the Red Cross program that I know for a fact that you just don't get in other courses. It's the best training program out there. But it was more for me. It was the first step. I've got a new lease on life, and I am sure not going to waste it."

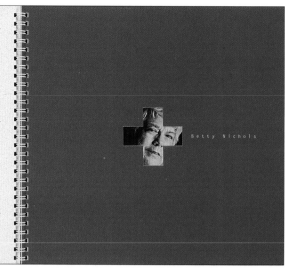

Betty Nichols

Grover Martin

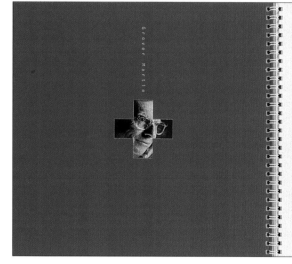

As a registered nurse, and instructor of the Red Cross "Foundation for Caring" Nursing Assistant program for the last five years, Betty Nichols has seen a lot of students. But not many that have overcome the obstacles Grover Martin encountered on the way to becoming one. When Grover entered Betty's class, he was 55, unemployed, and his life had taken just about every downward turn it could take, including a brush with death, but that didn't stop him. In fact, he was a really good student. According to Betty, "Someone who would keep coffee made and really paid attention in class." She says, "He always got to class early, and he seemed very eager to learn. He's worked hard and has been a tremendous success." Admittedly "Gung-Ho" about her class, Betty's enthusiasm toward caring for others helped provide Grover with the inspiration and the tools to change the direction of his life. And he's now on his way to becoming everything he wants to be. You can see quiet satisfaction in Betty's eyes when she says, "I'm very proud of Grover." And she should be. Because through Grover Martin, Betty has made a difference.

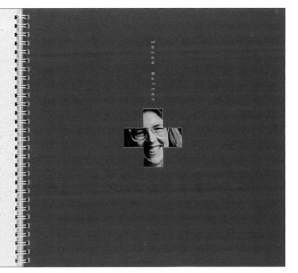

"Growing up, I was Miss Shelby County everything, I was popular, I was going to college, and I guess I thought I was too good to get my hands dirty." That's the way Marli Erwin remembers herself before she joined Red Cross. She admits, "I did it to compete for Miss Alabama. I needed a community service project, and Red Cross was it. You know, get in, fulfill the requirements, and get out. In fact, when they asked me to teach Scrubby Bears to children, I turned my nose up. I hated little kids!" Original intent aside, what resulted was a transition to adulthood. Both her mom and her Red Cross supervisor say Marli's attitude changed almost as soon as she started to teach the program, and two years later, she's still doing it. She says the most gratifying moment came when a little girl who had been in her swim safety class told of rescuing a friend with a life preserver. The child remembered to reach or throw and not to go. Marli recalled, "Because we teach them not to jump in after someone in trouble, she felt like a hero. And I taught her that. That is so neat."

Susan Walter is passionate about Red Cross Youth Services. Not only because she has twins at home, but because she feels that positive youth development is more important to our society than anything else she can think of. Once the American Red Cross Youth Director in Washington, D.C., Susan and her husband moved to Birmingham a few years ago. Now she's a volunteer with a mission. The biggest problem, she says, is that "So many kids aren't taught the value of putting others before themselves." Never was that more true than with youth volunteer and aspiring Miss Alabama contestant Marli Erwin, who just "needed some community service" under her belt. "What she got," Susan says "was a whole new set of priorities. That's part of what kids learn here. Youth volunteers work alongside our adult volunteers and share many of the same responsibilities. Plus, they get to work in any part of Red Cross that they choose. The kids see compassion for others. They learn how to lead, and more importantly, they learn how to give. Hopefully, that stays with them into adulthood."

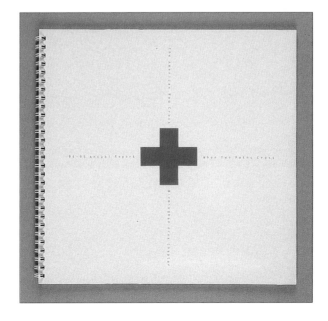

The Birmingham Area Chapter of the American Red Cross and Lewis Advertising developed this 1994-95 annual report on the theme "When Two Paths Cross," working from the premise that, as the arms of the Red Cross symbol intersect, so do the lives of the people that the organization brings together. Cross die-cuts between spreads are used to unite the photos of volunteers and people who were assisted by the Red Cross, with their stories told in the text surrounding the black-and-white images. The Red Cross had requested that the report be arranged according to the various services offered (Disaster, Blood, Youth, etc.), and Lewis Advertising designed computer collages put together from custom photography to illustrate divider pages for these sections. Service-specific financials are integrated within the main body of the report, while the general financials are printed on Kraft-paper colored stock. The main text is printed on S.D. Warren paper, and the report (which measures 10" x 10") has since been used as a Warren promotion.

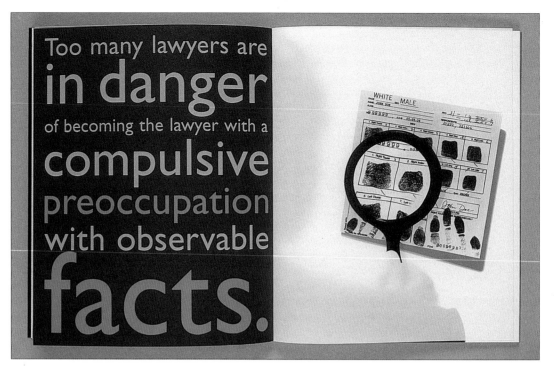

I hope three simple **words** can become the creed of new lawyers and the theme of my administration:

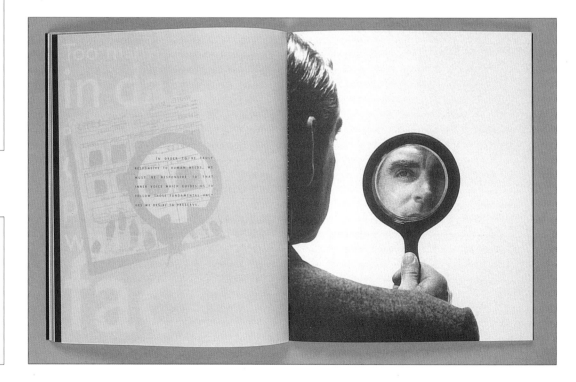

Design Firm:
Geer Design, Inc.,
Houston, Texas
Art Director:
Mark Geer
Designers:
Mark Geer, Mandy
Stewart
Illustrator:
Beryl Striewski

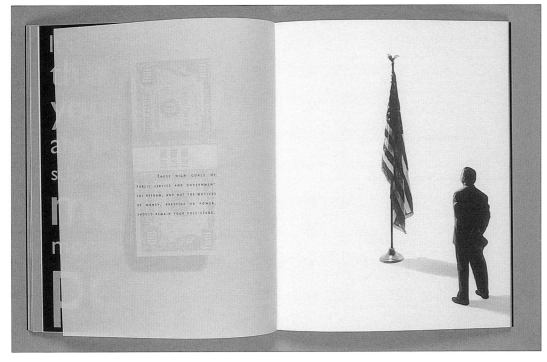

Each year, the Dean's Report of the South Texas College of Law provides financial information about the school and pays tribute to its donors. With a new dean taking the helm in 1995, that year's report also serves to commemorate his inauguration—and provides a manifesto for the future of the school in an era anxious for reform in the legal profession. Because the optimistic tone of the dean's installation address, reprinted as the text of this report, recalls the idealism of 1950s American commerce, icons that look like they might come from that era are used as illustrations. And to underscore the message of reform, vellum sheets inserted between spreads create before-and-after images: A lawyer scrutinizing fingerprints with a magnifying glass sees his own image in a mirror when the page is turned; another, standing before a stack of $100 bills, finds himself in front of an American flag, with text stating "public service and governmental reform, and not the motives of money, prestige or power, should remain your pole stars." The book measures 7 1/2" x 9 1/2".

All three insurance company annual reports in this section depend upon evocative rather than specific illustrations for visual impact. Keiler Design Group, in a book for Orion Capital Corporation (pp. 104–105), commissioned metaphorical images from David Wilcox to convey the company's reputation for problem solving in a fairly conventional manner. In contrast, the images for the other two reports radically reconfigure the annual report format for the insurance industry. The Progressive Corporation is well-known for its commitment to contemporary art, and its 1994 report, by Nesnadny+Schwartz, reinforces its interest in both art and diversity with silhouettes by Carter Kustera (pp. 106–107). While the imagery only tangentially relates to the field of insurance, it upholds the distinctive direction of this "progressive" company. The illustrations for the Zurich Reinsurance Centre annual report, on the other hand (this spread), were developed for a specific purpose —to demonstrate that reinsurance is "Not Boring," as the report is titled. Shots of foodstuffs were distorted by the photographer and cross-processed to achieve color saturation. The resulting images vibrate with an excitement generally foreign to the insurance field.

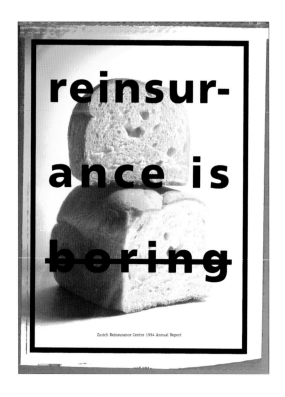

reinsur-
ance is
boring

Zurich Reinsurance Centre 1994 Annual Report

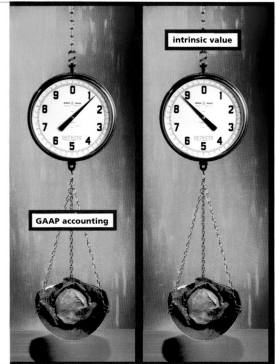

intrinsic value

GAAP accounting

Design Firm:
WYD Design,
Farmington, Connecticut
Art Directors:
James Pettus, Frank
Oswald, David
Dunkelberger
Designers:
James Pettus, Frank
Oswald
Photographers:
Christopher Hawker,
F. Scott Shafer
Copywriter:
Frank Oswald

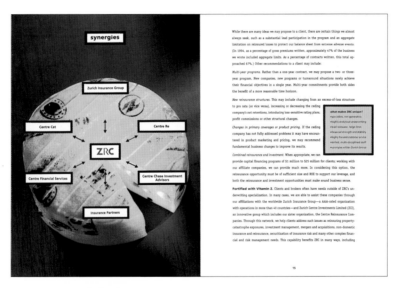

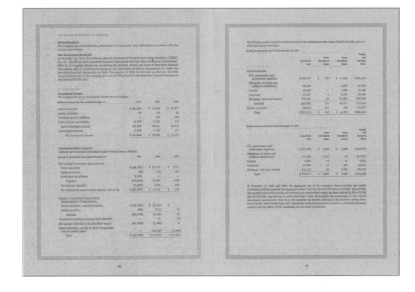

To combat the perception that the reinsurance industry is dull, WYD Design came up with "Not Boring," the 1994 annual report for Zurich Reinsurance Centre. This theme, and the "white bread" cover (measuring 8 3/4" x 11 3/4"), grew from the idea that ZRC products weren't commodities, enabling WYD Design to encapsulate the company's message in a single, poster-like image. The main design goal was to merge substance and style, combining smart but accessible text and graphs with completely unexpected graphics. (Even the financial highlights graphic was designed to look like a nutrition facts chart.) The cover image, a black-and-white stock shot obtained from Christopher Hawker, was colorized in Photoshop for a saturated, golden effect. The interior images of food products were shot by F. Scott Schafer. Most of the distortion was done with the camera, and cross processing was used to push the color saturation. The cover was printed with 4-color process inks plus an additional hit of black for the type and rule on Simpson Kashmir Kansas Cover, which has a texture that resembles bread. Interior pages, on Simpson Kashmir Book, were printed with specially formulated yellow and magenta inks with 25 per cent fluorescent inks.

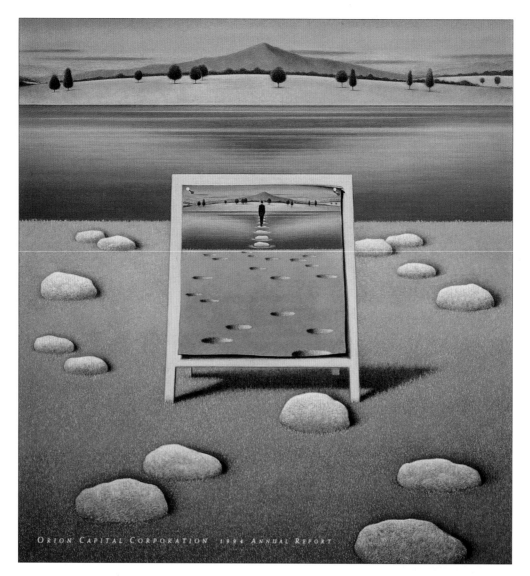

ORION CAPITAL CORPORATION 1994 ANNUAL REPORT

Design Firm:
Keiler Design Group,
Farmington, Connecticut
Creative Directors:
Mike Scricco, Mel Maffei
Art Director/Designer:
Chris Passehl
Illustrator:
David Wilcox
Copywriter:
Jeanne Hotchkiss

Letter to Shareholders

Dear Shareholder:

Once again we are pleased to report the results of a productive and profitable year. Operating earnings per share—the key measure of performance—increased 6.1% from $3.47 in 1993 to $3.68. Net premiums written in 1994 were up 12% from the 1993 level. And, against a backdrop of the seventh straight year of stiff price competition in the property and casualty insurance industry, we improved our combined ratio by two full percentage points. At 101.2%, that ratio beat the property and casualty insurance industry's result of 109.4%, as estimated by A.M. Best Company, by more than eight percentage points. We see room for additional improvement, but 1994's combined ratio is clearly outstanding for a company such as ours which emphasizes casualty lines.

The strength of our underwriting results led to a return on average equity for the year of a very respectable 14%, outpacing all but a few of our peers. In fact, in each of the last seven years our ROE has been at or above 14%, a record even fewer can report.

Our long-term performance success validates the inherent soundness of the operating strategy we put in place over a decade ago, and also, of course, validates its successful execution. At the heart of our strategy is a commitment to making a meaningful difference in the loss experience of our customers by working with them to design programs that meet their business objectives and have the potential to enhance their operations, as well as reduce costs and improve their profitability. We distinguish ourselves by the quality, focus, consistency and intensity of our services.

We expect to continue our record of strong returns on equity into 1995 and beyond. Such results are quite achievable, given the strength of our organization and culture, and the fact that we have had only minor exposure to catastrophes, pollution and toxic material liability—issues that have plagued many companies in our industry over the last several years.

As mentioned earlier, 1994's operating earnings per share increased 6.1%, to $3.68 per share on 14,348,000 average shares outstanding from $3.47 on 14,598,000 average shares outstanding, in 1993. Two special factors affected the year-to-year comparison. In 1994, our strong belief in our bright future led us to repurchase approximately 442,000 shares of our common stock in the open market, at an average cost of $31.08 per share, a move which positively impacted per share earnings. Also affecting the comparison, although in the opposite direction, was the fact that 1993's results were aided by an unusually high level of investment income. As discussed in last year's Annual Report, we benefited in 1993 from some timely real estate sales by certain limited partnerships in which we invested a few years ago. The real estate sales had a significantly larger impact on our earnings per share than did the share repurchases. Had investment income followed its long-term trend, the 6.1% increase in per share operating earnings for 1994 would have been substantially greater.

Operating earnings were $52,818,000 in 1994, compared with $51,100,000 in 1993. Net earnings were $55,245,000 and $68,813,000, or $3.85 per share and $4.69 per share, for the 1994 and 1993 years, respectively. In 1993, we recorded one-time benefits from the adoption of two new accounting standards which added $11,825,000, or $.81 per share, to net earnings. Also included in net earnings are after-tax realized investment gains of $2,427,000, or $.17 per share, in 1994, and $5,888,000, or $.41 per share, in 1993.

Growth at DPIC, EBI and SecurityRe brought Orion Capital's net premiums written to $712,055,000, from $635,586,000 in 1993. About half of the approximately $76 million premium volume rise came from our decision to increase DPIC's risk retention levels back to those that prevailed prior to 1991 by purchasing less reinsurance. The decision was a simple one, given the inherent profitability of DPIC's business and because of the strong capital position of our insurance operations. At the

Alan R. Gruber, Orion Chairman and Chief Executive Officer (foreground), and Larry D. Holler, President and Chief Operating Officer, are pictured in the new Mathematics, Computing and Engineering Center at Trinity College in Hartford, Connecticut. The building was designed by Cesar Pelli of New Haven, Connecticut, a long-time DPIC insured and recipient of the American Institute of Architects' 1995 Gold Medal for his success in integrating his buildings with their environments. Similarly, as specialists, Orion's understanding of our customers' businesses enables us to address their insurance problems with solutions that fit.

operations through geographic expansion and product extensions, as well as by tapping new market segments. Increased earnings potential exists not only in such growth, but also in the even greater margins that our loss reduction techniques can yield. Further we will seek out attractive acquisition candidates, those which can benefit from our focus, culture and management abilities.

In all of our growth efforts we are guided by the fundamental knowledge that we are making promises to pay claims in the future. We know that financial strength and prudence are keys to honoring our obligations. We are firm in our commitment that we will not grow just for growth's sake.

Our strategic and operational strengths are well supported by our skill in managing our capital, in balancing the needs of our operations for that capital — the raw material of our business — with delivering value to our shareholders and doing so at the lowest possible cost. And we are very good at making prudent, well-timed investments to enhance the bottom line.

Our continual efforts to deliver value to our customers, to maintain and adhere to disciplined underwriting standards, and to manage our finances in a savvy, judicious manner—all are directed toward rewarding our shareholders. Our continued superior performance in shareholder return reflects this focus and our ability to deliver upon it. A broadly-held understanding of what builds

value drives our commitment and our confidence in Orion's future.

EBI COMPANIES

Workers Compensation

In 1994, even though the overall workers compensation industry recorded sharply improved results, EBI continued to significantly outpace the industry's performance. It was the sixth consecutive year it has done so. At 90.1%, EBI's combined ratio for 1994 was nearly nine points better than the 99% estimated by A.M. Best Company for the workers compensation industry.

EBI's approach to workers compensation insurance is one of being highly selective, highly specialized and intensely involved in each account. It strives to change the work environments and work practices of each of its insureds, to prevent on-the-job injuries and lower claims costs. In this way, EBI has transformed what has long been a commodity insurance coverage.

EBI targets mid-sized businesses and service establishments (such as nursing homes and hospitals)—in particular those which have had problems controlling their workers compensation costs. These insureds are generally small enough not to have risk management staffs of their own, but large enough to justify, and benefit from, EBI's cost-reduction services.

Effective workers compensation cost control obviously starts with reducing the

number and severity of worker injuries. EBI teams up with its insureds and agents, to help identify and understand what has been driving such costs up. Then EBI helps develop and successfully implement plans to reduce those cost drivers.

When injuries do happen, EBI emphasizes getting workers the best medical care available, knowing that to do so serves the best interests of the workers, and helps reduce costs by getting people back to productive employment as soon as possible.

The greatest potential, however, lies in preventing all lost-time injuries. EBI's increasing emphasis on building a Zero Accident Culture in each insured's workplace reflects the ultimate rewards of such thinking. By rejecting the conventional wisdom that accidents are inevitable, EBI, its policyholders and their employees build ever-lengthening periods of injury-free operation, and even greater performance gains.

More often than not, EBI customers reap not only workers compensation cost savings, but benefits in productivity and product quality as well. High levels of customer loyalty are a result of EBI's responsive services. Such customer satisfaction, and the reputation that it produces, helped EBI increase written premiums by more than 10% last year, both through greater penetration of existing markets and through controlled market expansion. Earnings also increased dramatically as customer losses—and EBI's costs—were reduced.

EBI remains selective about the states in which it operates, looking for stable regul-

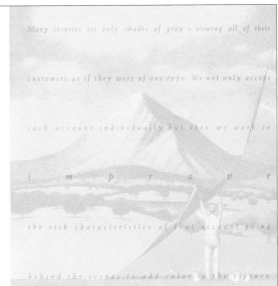

ships with the very best reinsurance intermediaries: in claims, financial services and data processing, as well as underwriting. This process is enhanced by the company's lack of bureaucracy and by the commitment of everyone on the SecurityRe team to provide first class service. SecurityRe distinguishes itself by investing the time required on every proposal it receives to fully understand the underlying reinsurance needs and the reinsurance program being presented. Significant too is the company's deep appreciation of the fact that the regional companies and specialty companies which are SecurityRe's principal clients depend upon efficient and unencumbered service to maintain their own competitive positions.

Control — not just of individual exposures, but of overall risk portfolio balance and expenses — is an essential underpinning of SecurityRe's strategy. Each of these elements has a direct bearing on the others, and on SecurityRe's ability to maintain operating continuity — as well as on the flexibility to take full advantage of favorable market conditions and to preserve those gains when conditions deteriorate. This focus and discipline has enabled SecurityRe to outperform the broker market industry segment, the one in which it competes, by an average of more than four combined ratio points since 1979, the year in which SecurityRe was formed.

SecurityRe operates nationally and concentrates the majority of its business in casualty lines. Four years ago, the company began a conscious effort to reduce its property catastrophe exposures, a move that was subsequently followed by many other broker market companies. SecurityRe remains a property market on a selective basis, writing excess-of-loss coverage when it can define and understand the exposures it is assuming. Consequently, the company has had relatively small exposure to catastrophe losses. (The Northridge Earthquake, which cost the industry over $11 billion, cost SecurityRe less than $1 million.) Automobile liability business, which has a short loss development tail, comprises better than half of the company's treaty reinsurance portfolio.

The careful way in which SecurityRe has built its business exemplifies its long-term commitment to the reinsurance marketplace, and to its own bottom line performance. With primary market pricing weak and prospects for firmer reinsurance rates dim, 1995 market conditions are especially challenging. SecurityRe will maintain its range of products, and direct its efforts to those niches where profit margins and terms are attractive. The skill, experience, service and focus of SecurityRe's people define the company and equip it to meet the challenges and opportunities of the reinsurance market with continuing success.

NATIONS' CARE

Alternative Market Workers Compensation

Nations' Care began operation in late 1993 with all the youthful exuberance of a fledgling organization and all the savvy of a seasoned veteran. A new Orion operating company literally carved out of a well-established market leader (EBI), Nations' Care is testimony to one of Orion's most powerful instincts: to seek out opportunity and seize it.

With the establishment of Nations' Care, Orion has effectively extended the continuum on which it can function for its customers as a leading provider of workers compensation and related services. In effect, Nations' Care applies the loss prevention and claims management techniques developed by EBI to help effect risk reduction and long-term cost control for businesses which prefer to self-fund all or a portion (through large policy deductibles) of their workers compensation exposures, as well as for those who seek to integrate their workers compensation and group health program administration. These customers are typically larger than EBI's mainstream accounts.

The approach taken by Nations' Care is comprehensive and integrated.

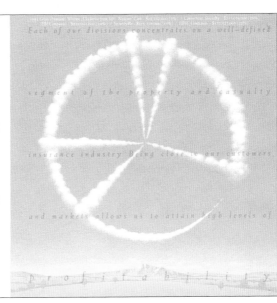

In its 1994 annual report, Orion Capital Corporation, a property and casualty insurance company, wanted to spotlight its reputation as a problem-solver in niche markets where its skills are best utilized. Keiler Design Group chose dramatic, conceptual illustrations by David Wilcox to tell Orion's story in this 9 1/8" x 10" book. Vellum sheets positioned over the illustrations are printed with text linking the witty yet refined images to the company's message. Retiring president and vice chairman Robert Sanborn is photographed at the Boston Garden, and Celtic green makes a number of appearances in this book—mainly for the financial pages and the ink for the numbers.

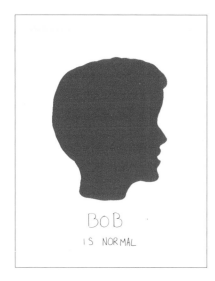

BOB
IS NORMAL

Design Firm:
Nesnadny+Schwartz,
Cleveland, Ohio
Art Directors:
Mark Schwartz, Joyce
Nesnadny
Designers:
Mark Schwartz, Michelle
Moehler, Joyce Nesnadny
Illustrator:
Carter Kustera

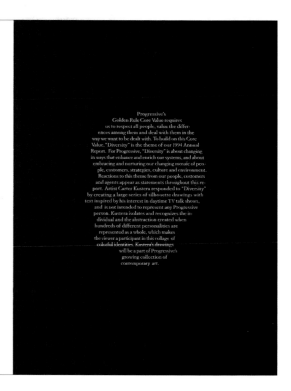

Diversity
reminds me
of the art
of pointillism:
perfect
individual dots
up close;
blurred images
from five
paces back;
remarkable
clarity
of each point's
purpose
and
value from the
intended
perspective.

Progressive's
Golden Rule Core Value requires
us to respect all people, value the differences among them and deal with them in the
way we want to be dealt with. To build on this Core
Value, "Diversity" is the theme of our 1994 Annual
Report. For Progressive, "Diversity" is about changing
in ways that enhance and enrich our systems, and about
embracing and nurturing our changing mosaic of people, customers, strategies, culture and environment.
Reactions to this theme from our people, customers
and agents appear as statements throughout this report. Artist Carter Kustera responded to "Diversity"
by creating a large series of silhouette drawings with
text inspired by his interest in daytime TV talk shows,
and is not intended to represent any Progressive
person. Kustera isolates and recognizes the individual and the abstraction created when
hundreds of different personalities are
represented as a whole, which makes
the viewer a participant in this collage of
colorful identities. Kustera's drawings
will be a part of Progressive's
growing collection of
contemporary art.

It is important
to define ,
Progressive's
understanding
of the term diversity.
It is difficult
to embrace a concept
many of us
do not
understand.

About Progressive: The Progressive
insurance organization began business in 1937. Progressive Casualty Insurance Company was founded in
1956. The Progressive Corporation, an
insurance holding company formed in
1965, owns 60 operating subsidiaries
and has one mutual insurance company affiliate. The companies provide
personal automobile insurance and
other specialty property-casualty insurance and related services sold pri-
marily through independent insurance
agents in the United States and
Canada. The 1994 estimated industry
premiums, which include personal
auto insurance in the U.S. and Ontario,
Canada, as well as insurance for commercial vehicles, were $119 billion and
Progressive's share was 2.0 percent.

DANIEL
WENT FROM SECRETARY TO
HEAD OF DEPARTMENT IN 3 WEEKS

AARON

IS JUST HAPPY TO BE ALIVE

BEATRICE

CLAIMS SHE CAN COMMUNICATE WITH THE DEAD

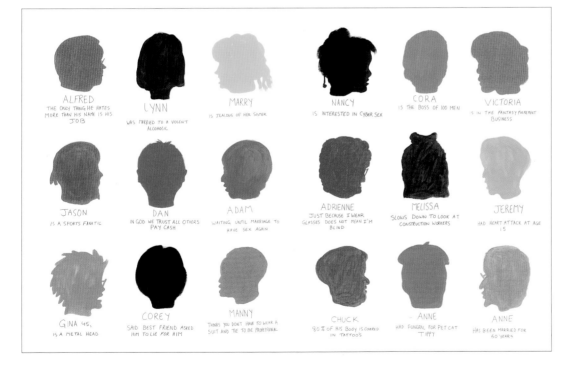

ALFRED
THE ONLY THING HE HATES MORE THAN HIS NAME IS HIS JOB

LYNN
WAS MARRIED TO A VIOLENT ALCOHOLIC

MARRY
IS JEALOUS OF HER SISTER

NANCY
IS INTERESTED IN CYBER SEX

CORA
IS THE BOSS OF 100 MEN

VICTORIA
IS IN THE FANTASY PAYMENT BUSINESS

JASON
IS A SPORTS FANATIC

DAN
IN GOD WE TRUST ALL OTHERS PAY CASH

ADAM
WAITING UNTIL MARRIAGE TO HAVE SEX AGAIN

ADRIENNE
JUST BECAUSE I WEAR GLASSES DOES NOT MEAN I'M BLIND

MELISSA
SLOWS DOWN TO LOOK AT CONSTRUCTION WORKERS

JEREMY
HAD HEART ATTACK AT AGE 15

GINA 45,
IS A METAL HEAD

COREY
SAID BEST FRIEND ASKED HIM TO LIE FOR HIM

MANNY
THINKS YOU DON'T HAVE TO WEAR A SUIT AND TIE TO BE PROFESSIONAL

CHUCK
80% OF HIS BODY IS COVERED IN TATTOOS

ANNE
HAD FUNERAL FOR PET CAT TIPPY

ANNE
HAS BEEN MARRIED FOR 60 YEARS

The Progressive Corporation, an insurance holding company, is well-known for its commitment to and collection of contemporary art. The company chose the theme of "Diversity" for its 1994 annual report and asked its employees, customers, and independent agents to share their thoughts about the ways that differences can enhance and enrich. Nesnadny+Schwartz commissioned contemporary artist Carter Kustera to respond to the theme in visual terms. Kustera created a series of silhouette drawings with text that reflects TV talk show discourse. To echo the many colors of Kustera's heads, some spreads feature quotes on the concept of "diversity" printed in multi-colored type. The 8 1/2" x 11" book is perfect bound. The Mead Sig-Nature Satin cover sports an embossed stamp, with offline letterpress scores on face hinges, and alternating blocks of color on the spine. The financial pages, printed on French Dur-O-Tone Butcher stock in various shades of green and lavender, continue the diversity motif.

While many design firms creating annual reports face the problem of producing something entertaining out of the stuff of board meetings, Leimer Cross Design experienced the opposite in its book for Nintendo (pp. 110–111): expressing serious business concerns about the stuff of entertainment. Sharp focus, glossy photos of equipment and original digital art depicting Nintendo characters present a year that saw a 14 per cent decline in consolidated net sales in a positive light. Petrick Design's book for radio group Jacor Communications (this spread) attempts to pass itself off as an ordinary annual report with a sober cover treatment, but the pun in its coverline—"1994 was a sound year for Jacor"—hints at the fun found within. The "sound year" is recounted not in a serious shareholders' letter, but on an audio CD set in a die-cut within the text. Financials printed in red ink on fluorescent red paper carry Jacor's irreverent attitude to a radical extreme.

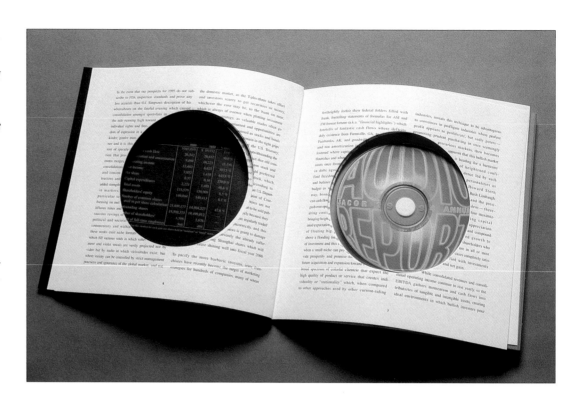

Design Firm:
Petrick Design,
Chicago, Illinois
Art Director:
Robert Petrick
Designers:
Robert Petrick,
Laura Ress

1994 WAS A SOUND YEAR FOR JACOR

The 1994 annual report for Jacor Communications, the nation's eighth largest radio group, contains all the legally required financial information—but its resemblance to the average annual report stops there. Because "Jacor is not your average radio company," Petrick Design was challenged to create a not-so-average—even irreverent—annual report. The cover was created to suggest business as usual: an 8 1/2" square of Simpson Starwhite Vicksburg, with a letterpressed cover line. Open it, though, and you find an "audio report," on CD, set within the die-cut pages. The only visual for this annual report, in fact, is the Photoshop-created, silkscreened lettering on the CD itself. While the letter to shareholders is (reasonably) straightforward, and legible despite the die-cut, the "Notes of Interest" that follow—14 pages of them—offer gems like "We believe that radio systems systematically must sustain symphony and saxophone savorers alike by shoring up sexy advertising..." The financial pages are serious, at least in terms of actual numbers. That they're printed in red ink on red-pink Hopper Hots stock demonstrates just how far Jacor and Petrick were willing to go in the creation of something truly unique in the world of annual reports.

JACOR COMMUNICATIONS, INC.

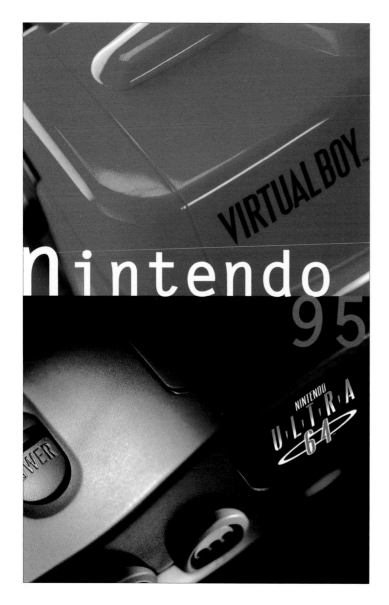

VIRTUAL BOY™

Nintendo 95

NINTENDO ULTRA 64

The first three dimensional moving pictures for your home. The first interface... around your face. Another way. Another world.

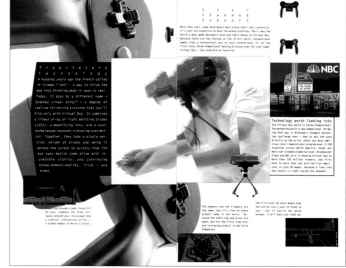

NBC

Game Boy

Design Firm:
Leimer Cross Design,
Seattle, Washington
Art Director/Designer:
Kerry Leimer
Photographer:
Tyler Boley

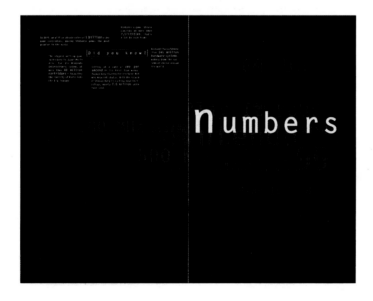

The main problem for Leimer Cross Design in creating the 1995 annual report for Nintendo, the Kyoto-based interactive entertainment company, was to represent all existing and new product lines in an engaging, accessible format. Leimer Cross chose to combine hardware, software, and character art in discrete, platform-driven sections, like the well-known Game Boy, and the new Virtual Boy, which provides the player with "3D immersion." Because products like Virtual Boy and Ultra 64 (the first home video game system with true 64-bit processing) depend on superior visuals for their appeal, screen-grabs illustrate the games, along with original digital art that showcases the characters that have made Nintendo famous. While a somewhat subdued letter from the president, printed in gray on Potlatch Elegance, opens the 7 1/2" x 12" book, glossy pages use blocks of black set on white to set off the colorful vibrancy of the Nintendo experience.

Both of the annual reports for transportation and shipping industries that follow express a similar message—getting people or products to their destinations as quickly and inexpensively as possible—with widely divergent means. Southwest, "the low fare airline," as it bills itself, uses LUV as its stock exchange symbol, to represent its base at Dallas Love Field, "as well as the theme of our Employee and Customer relationships." The airline's friendly mission, however, is not represented by images of happy employees and clients, but rather, through cute, children's book–like visuals, in a report by Sibley/Peteet Design (this spread). The Expeditors International annual report, by Leimer Cross Design, also emphasizes employee/client communication, through both technological and human channels. The Expeditors book, though, suggests streamlining and an all-business mentality through a sleek black-and-white presentation (pp. 114–115).

Design Firm:
Sibley/Peteet Design, Austin, Texas
Art Directors:
Tim McClure, Rex C. Peteet
Designers:
Rex C. Peteet, Matt Heck, K. C. Teis
Illustrator:
Peter Kramer
Agency:
GSD&M

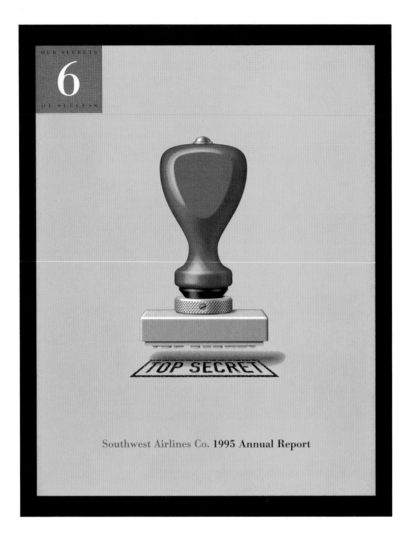

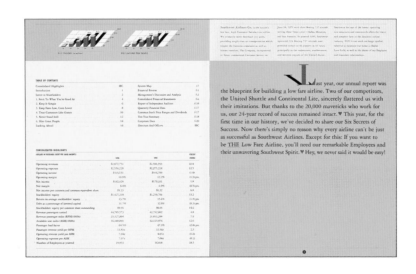

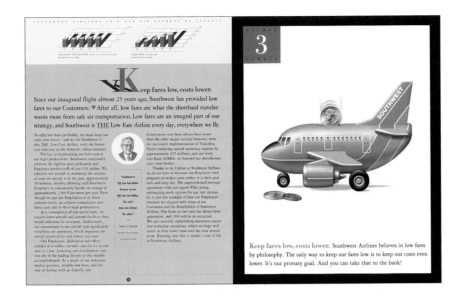

Keep fares low, costs lower. Southwest Airlines believes in low fares by philosophy. The only way to keep our fares low is to keep our costs even lower. It's our primary goal. And you can take that to the bank!

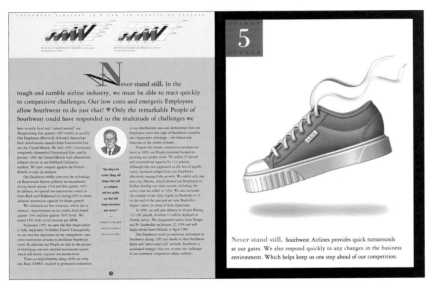

Never stand still. Southwest Airlines provides quick turnarounds at our gates. We also respond quickly to any changes in the business environment. Which helps keep us one step ahead of our competition.

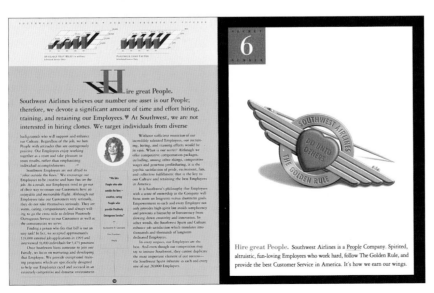

Hire great People. Southwest Airlines is a People Company. Spirited, altruistic, fun-loving Employees who work hard, follow The Golden Rule, and provide the best Customer Service in America. It's how we earn our wings.

The 1994 annual report for Southwest Airlines offered a blueprint for "how to build a low fare airline." After a couple of competitors took the advice, the logical theme for the 1995 report, created by Sibley/Peteet Design, was "how to build *the* low fare airline." This is done by sharing Southwest's six "secrets" for success: Stick to what you're good at; Keep it simple; Keep fares low, costs lower; Treat customers like guests; Never stand still; and Hire great people. The company maintains that their success cannot be imitated because their secrets cannot be implemented by anyone other than Southwest's "remarkable employees." These "secrets" are built upon the kind of golden-rule concepts taught in grade school, and their accompanying digital images (designed by Sibley/Peteet and rendered by Peter Kramer of Dusseldorf, Germany) are appropriately simple, bright, and fun. These ideas and images are also in keeping with Southwest's low-cost, casual style. Special ink mixes in high-key colors on uncoated Mohawk Options stock continue the impression of a kid's activity book rather than a numbingly conventional financial document. The piece measures 8 3/8" x 10 7/8".

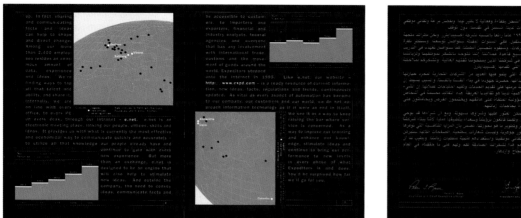

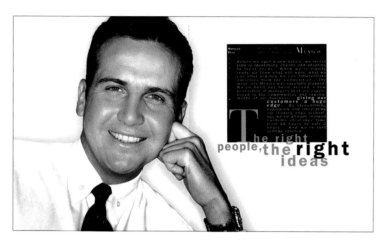

people, the right **right**
ideas

You can never
be close **enough to**
your
customer

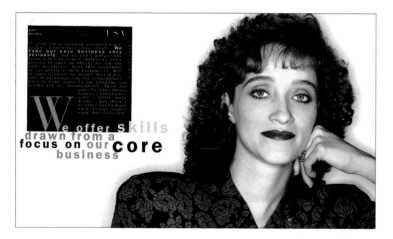

We offer **Skills**
drawn from a
focus on our **core**
business

Proving that
we make a
difference
in **new**
markets

Design Firm:
Leimer Cross Design,
Seattle, Washington
Art Director/Designer:
Kerry Leimer
Illustrator:
Tyler Boley

Expeditors International, a logistics company, wanted to focus on improvements to its information systems in its 1995 annual report. Leimer Cross Design stylishly reinforces the Expeditors' ability to communicate with customers and agencies worldwide with this 7 1/2" x 9" book, conceived mainly in black-and-white. (The only touches of bright color appear in the chairman/CEO's signature, in blue; and the Expeditors logo on the back cover, in red.) The first third of the book contains the letter to shareholders and a description of the company's information systems, illustrated with maps and graphs. The text, repeated in five languages, is printed on black stock. The second section is devoted to the people of Expeditors, handsomely portrayed in full-page photos, accompanied by personal comments set in black text boxes. The third section, the financials, is printed on white stock.

EXPEDITORS INTERNATIONAL

Consolidated Statements of Earnings — IN THOUSANDS, EXCEPT SHARE DATA — YEARS ENDED DECEMBER 31.	1995	1994	1993
REVENUES:			
AIRFREIGHT	$407,188	315,646	259,172
OCEAN FREIGHT	126,638	92,945	74,859
CUSTOMS BROKERAGE AND IMPORT SERVICES	50,865	42,116	27,456
TOTAL REVENUES	584,691	450,607	361,487
OPERATING EXPENSES:			
AIRFREIGHT CONSOLIDATION	334,281	257,994	208,666
OCEAN FREIGHT CONSOLIDATION	96,337	73,473	59,398
SALARIES AND RELATED COSTS	84,272	64,177	50,104
SELLING AND PROMOTION	7,545	5,293	4,021
RENT	6,651	5,563	3,881
DEPRECIATION AND AMORTIZATION	6,629	4,919	3,692
OTHER	22,125	17,834	15,409
TOTAL OPERATING EXPENSES	557,840	429,253	345,170
OPERATING INCOME	26,851	21,354	16,317
OTHER INCOME (EXPENSE):			
INTEREST EXPENSE	(312)	(199)	(249)
INTEREST INCOME	1,741	1,273	1,061
OTHER, NET	119	(40)	(60)
OTHER INCOME, NET	1,548	1,034	752
EARNINGS BEFORE INCOME TAXES	28,399	22,388	17,069
INCOME TAX EXPENSE	11,004	9,171	6,902
NET EARNINGS	$ 17,395	13,217	10,167
NET EARNINGS PER COMMON SHARE	$ 1.36	$ 1.08	$ .85
WEIGHTED AVERAGE SHARES OUTSTANDING	12,583,078	12,275,117	12,025,890

See accompanying notes to consolidated financial statements.

EXPEDITORS INTERNATIONAL OF WASHINGTON, INC. 42

Consolidated Statements of Shareholders' Equity — IN THOUSANDS, EXCEPT SHARE DATA — YEARS ENDED DECEMBER 31, 1995, 1994 AND 1993	Common Stock		Additional Paid-In Capital	Retained Earnings	Equity Adjustments from Foreign Currency Translation	Total
	Shares	Par Value				
BALANCE AT DECEMBER 31, 1992	11,795,642	$118	11,840	63,960	3,075	78,993
EXERCISE OF STOCK OPTIONS	3,350	–	30	–	–	30
ISSUANCE OF SHARES UNDER STOCK PURCHASE PLAN	41,688	–	452	–	–	452
TAX BENEFITS RELATED TO STOCK OPTIONS AND STOCK PURCHASE PLAN	–	–	7	–	–	7
NET EARNINGS	–	–	–	10,167	–	10,167
FOREIGN CURRENCY TRANSLATION ADJUSTMENTS	–	–	–	–	(826)	(826)
DIVIDENDS PAID ($.10 PER SHARE)	–	–	–	(1,182)	–	(1,182)
BALANCE AT DECEMBER 31, 1993	11,840,680	$118	12,329	72,945	2,249	87,641
EXERCISE OF STOCK OPTIONS, NET	154,340	2	1,622	–	–	1,624
ISSUANCE OF SHARES UNDER STOCK PURCHASE PLAN	50,999	–	556	–	–	556
SHARES REPURCHASED UNDER PROVISIONS OF STOCK REPURCHASE PLAN	(111,176)	(1)	(2,172)	–	–	(2,173)
TAX BENEFITS RELATED TO STOCK OPTIONS AND STOCK PURCHASE PLAN	–	–	316	–	–	316
NET EARNINGS	–	–	–	13,217	–	13,217
FOREIGN CURRENCY TRANSLATION ADJUSTMENTS, NET OF DEFERRED TAXES OF $196	–	–	–	–	1,120	1,120
DIVIDENDS PAID ($.10 PER SHARE)	–	–	–	(1,191)	–	(1,191)
BALANCE AT DECEMBER 31, 1994	11,934,843	$119	12,651	84,971	3,369	101,110
EXERCISE OF STOCK OPTIONS, NET	96,520	1	1,143	–	–	1,144
ISSUANCE OF SHARES UNDER STOCK PURCHASE PLAN	60,423	1	989	–	–	990
SHARES REPURCHASED UNDER PROVISIONS OF STOCK REPURCHASE PLAN	(81,123)	(1)	(2,062)	–	–	(2,063)
TAX BENEFITS RELATED TO STOCK OPTIONS AND STOCK PURCHASE PLAN	–	–	408	–	–	408
NET EARNINGS	–	–	–	17,395	–	17,395
FOREIGN CURRENCY TRANSLATION ADJUSTMENTS, NET OF DEFERRED TAX CREDIT OF $196	–	–	–	–	(354)	(354)
DIVIDENDS PAID ($.12 PER SHARE)	–	–	–	(1,438)	–	(1,438)
BALANCE AT DECEMBER 31, 1995	12,010,663	$120	13,129	100,928	3,015	117,192

See accompanying notes to consolidated financial statements.

EXPEDITORS INTERNATIONAL OF WASHINGTON, INC. 43

Representing abstract computer and information solution services in annual reports is no easy task. The accomplishments of the MRJ Group are symbolized through images of the people and organizations they've assisted, like an FBI agent at his computer, or a NASA space shuttle (p. 122). Edward Walter Design commissioned Jack Unruh to depict MRJ's history in the form of a fold-out timeline. Reports for Rational Software Corporation and Oak Technology focus on specific concepts to help convey abstract services. For Rational Software (this spread), Cahan & Associates brought in Jeffrey Fisher to paint simplified, accessible visuals showing how microprocessors can be found in everyday products. In Oak Technnology's book (pp. 118–119), Cahan went with images taken from CDs, in order to feature a product specifically enabled by Oak's CD-ROM controllers. In contrast to the above companies, Fluke Corporation manufactures products—professional electronic test tools—that are literally "hands-on." These products form the basis of Leimer Cross Design's annual report for Fluke: the tools, their uses, and the ultimate effect on the everyday person, are featured in spreads (pp. 120–121).

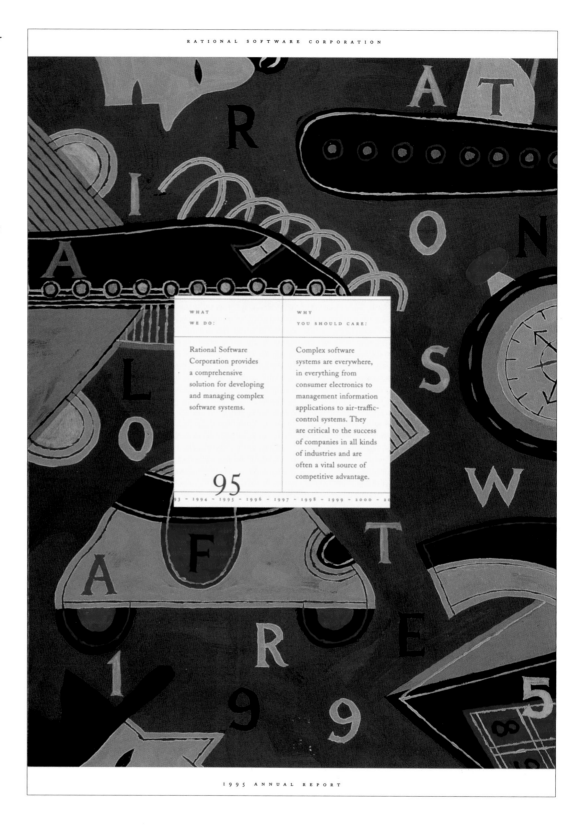

Design Firm:
Cahan & Associates,
San Francisco, California
Art Directors:
Bob Dinetz, Bill Cahan
Illustrator:
Jeffrey Fisher/Riley
Illustration

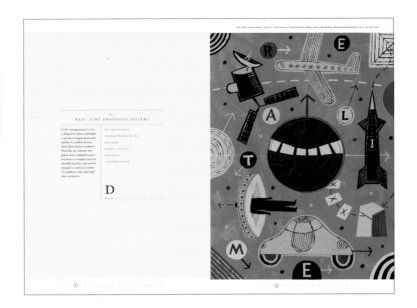

Rational
Corporation assists cus-
tomers in developing and
maintaining complex soft-
ware systems. The goal of its
1995 annual report,
designed by Cahan &
Associates, was to explain
exactly what Rational
does—and why anyone
should care. To this end,
accessible, consumer-ori-
ented images were commis-
sioned from Jeffrey Fisher to
engage the reader in this
difficult-to-explain area of
expertise, and to display the
ubiquity of microprocessors
in products around the
world. Fisher's hand-painted
illustrations also play a role
in de-emphasizing Rational's
government and defense
work of the past, while highlighting the company's current involvement in everyday consumer products.
Spreads featuring easy-to-
understand two-color
graphs help to explain
Rational's business mission.
Certain pieces of information, like key words and
page numbers, are pre-
sented in time-line style,
with the appropriate word
or number highlighted, in
order to symbolically
acknowledge the company's
past as it works to improve
the future. The book
measures 8 1/4" x 11 3/4".

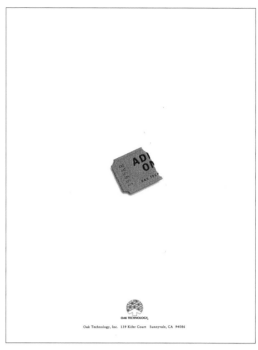

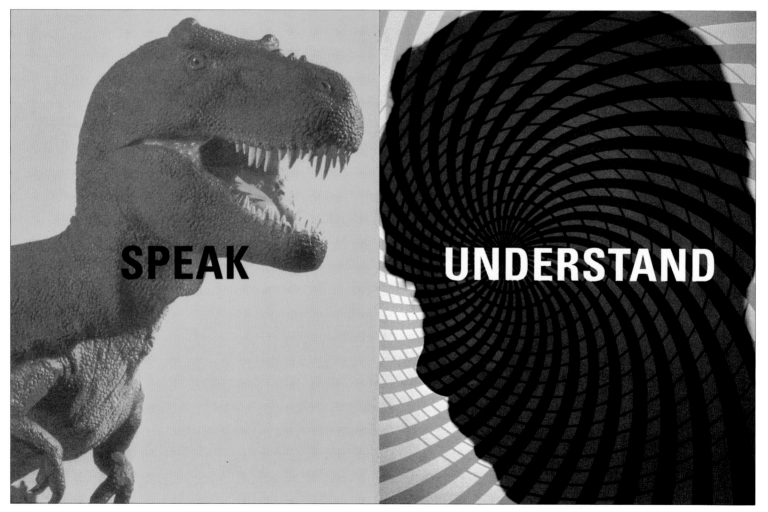

Design Firm:
Cahan & Associates,
San Francisco, California
Art Director:
Bill Cahan
Designer:
Craig Clark

TO OUR STOCKHOLDERS: OAK TECHNOLOGY ACHIEVED SEVERAL IMPORTANT MILESTONES IN FISCAL 1995, CLEARLY THE BEST YEAR IN OUR COMPANY'S HISTORY: REVENUES EXCEEDED $100 MILLION FOR THE FIRST TIME. TOTAL SALES OF OUR CD-ROM CONTROLLERS TOPPED 10 MILLION DURING THE YEAR. OAK IS CURRENTLY THE WORLD'S LARGEST MERCHANT SUPPLIER OF CD-ROM CONTROLLERS. OAK BECAME A PUBLIC COMPANY IN FEBRUARY, AND RAISED ADDITIONAL CAPITAL WITH A FOLLOW-ON OFFERING IN MAY. WE COMPLETED OUR FIRST GUARANTEED CAPACITY AGREEMENT WITH A KEY SEMICONDUCTOR FOUNDRY AND ARE PURSUING ADDITIONAL ARRANGEMENTS.

PERCEIVE

LISTEN

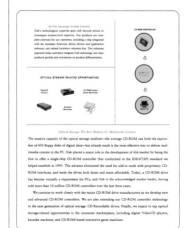

INTERACTIVE MULTIMEDIA HAS FOSTERED NEW TRENDS IN EDUCATION, ENTERTAINMENT AND BUSINESS. IT HAS ALSO LED TO NEW METHODS TO DELIVER AND ACCESS INFORMATION. OPTICAL STORAGE TECHNOLOGY HAS MADE DELIVERING MULTIMEDIA CONTENT INEXPENSIVE AND EFFECTIVE.

Oak Technology is a leading supplier of high-performance, comprehensive semiconductor and software solutions that fuel the development of interactive multimedia. When the company initially approached Cahan & Associates for the design of its 1995 annual report, it requested a conservative book that would blend in with those of the competition. Cahan, however, convinced Oak that the best way to change the financial community's false belief it was a one-product company and to explain Oak's technology was to convey the excitement of multimedia with offbeat word and image juxtapositions and aggressive typography. The ticket on the cover can be removed; underneath, it reads, "Oak Technology: Your Ticket to Interactive Media." The first eight pages of the 8 1/2" x 11" book are image only. Because Oak is the world's largest merchant supplier of CD-ROM controllers, these images are taken from a variety of CD sources, like Voyager, FPG, and Photonica. A two-page profile follows; then, an operations review. In an unusual step, Cahan persuaded Oak to run the shareholder's letter immediately before the financials, rather than at the beginning of the book, on the theory that people would flip through from back to front.

OAK TECHNOLOGY

Design Firm:
Leimer Cross Design,
Seattle, Washington
Art Director/Designer:
Kerry Leimer
Photographer:
Jeff Corwin

53rd floor – biggest meeting of the year. The elevators are running because the Fluke 865 Graphical MultiMeter makes preventative maintenance accurate and easy. **No complaints from the tenants.** And reaching the meeting on time was easy.

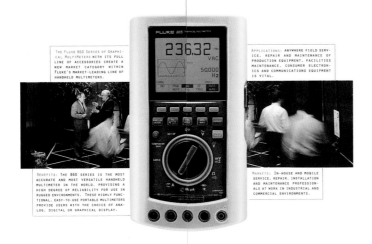

THE FLUKE 860 SERIES OF GRAPHI-
CAL MULTIMETERS WITH ITS FULL
LINE OF ACCESSORIES CREATE A
NEW MARKET CATEGORY WITHIN
FLUKE'S MARKET-LEADING LINE OF
HANDHELD MULTIMETERS.

APPLICATIONS: ANYWHERE FIELD SERV-
ICE, REPAIR AND MAINTENANCE OF
PRODUCTION EQUIPMENT, FACILITIES
MAINTENANCE, CONSUMER ELECTRON-
ICS AND COMMUNICATIONS EQUIPMENT
IS VITAL.

BENEFITS: THE 860 SERIES IS THE MOST
ACCURATE AND MOST VERSATILE HANDHELD
MULTIMETER IN THE WORLD, PROVIDING A
HIGH DEGREE OF RELIABILITY FOR USE IN
RUGGED ENVIRONMENTS. THESE HIGHLY FUNC-
TIONAL, EASY-TO-USE PORTABLE MULTIMETERS
PROVIDE USERS WITH THE CHOICE OF ANA-
LOG, DIGITAL OR GRAPHICAL DISPLAY.

MARKETS: IN-HOUSE AND MOBILE
SERVICE, REPAIR, INSTALLATION
AND MAINTENANCE PROFESSION-
ALS AT WORK IN INDUSTRIAL AND
COMMERCIAL ENVIRONMENTS.

Your car dealership – the technician has just fixed the electronic fuel injection system in your new car using a Fluke 98 Automotive ScopeMeter. **It saved him 30 minutes.** It saved your vacation.

THE FLUKE 98 AUTOMOTIVE SCOPEMETER WITH
ITS COMPREHENSIVE LINE OF AUTOMOTIVE
ACCESSORIES COMPLEMENTS FLUKE'S EXIST-
ING LINE OF HANDHELD AUTOMOTIVE METERS,
THE STANDARD OF EXCELLENCE IN THE AU-
TOMOTIVE INDUSTRY.

APPLICATIONS: MAINTENANCE AND
TROUBLESHOOTING FOR AUTOMOTIVE
ELECTRONIC SYSTEMS SUCH AS EN-
GINE CONTROLS, ANTI-LOCK BRAKE
SYSTEMS, ELECTRONIC TRANSMISSIONS
AND CLIMATE CONTROL SYSTEMS.

BENEFITS: THE FASTEST, SIMPLEST WAY
TO MEASURE AND DISPLAY AUTOMOTIVE
ELECTRONIC SIGNALS, EVEN THOSE TYPI-
CAL OF TRICKY INTERMITTENT PROBLEMS.
TRUE PORTABILITY MAKES FLUKE AUTO-
MOTIVE SCOPEMETERS INDISPENSABLE FOR
BOTH ROAD TESTS AND SHOP WORK.

MARKETS: AUTOMOTIVE TECH-
NICIANS WORKING IN DEAL-
ERSHIPS, INDEPENDENT REPAIR
SHOPS, TUNE-UP AND EMIS-
SIONS SHOPS FOR EVERY MAKE,
AROUND THE WORLD.

The 1995 annual report for the Fluke Corporation, makers of compact, professional electronic test tools, takes its 6 3/8" x 11" shape and color palette (mainly black, white, and yellow) from one of Fluke's products, the ScopeMeter pictured on the cover. Leimer Cross Design's assignment was to demonstrate the value of the company to a non-technical audience. This is achieved by constructing spreads around color photographs of specific products, illustrating (in duotones) and emphasizing (in bright and direct text) their impact on everyday life. For example, the ScopeMeter, which measures and analyzes voltages and currents in avionics systems, is shown alongside typical airport scenes, with text explaining that, because the avionics technician is using a Fluke ScopeMeter, "Your flight leaves right on time." The Fluke CEO and president are portrayed in black-and-white photographs, surrounded by company products.

MRJ GROUP, INC.

MRJ Group provides state-of-the-art solutions to the most technically and economically challenging problems facing customers in fields such as aerospace engineering and high-performance computing. Edward Walter Design produced this 1995 annual report with a company history timeline in the form of a pull-out poster that can also be distributed as a stand-alone piece. The designer chose Jack Unruh to illustrate it, not only for his distinctively warm style and use of handwriting (both suitable for this employee-owned company), but also because "he's a wonderful personality." The timeline was created in two pieces on illustration board at a size larger than the report itself (8" x 11"). It was thus unscannable and had to be shot in 8" x 10" transparencies and rejoined by the separator. The accordion-fold poster and the removable glue strip to hold it in place were also binding challenges.

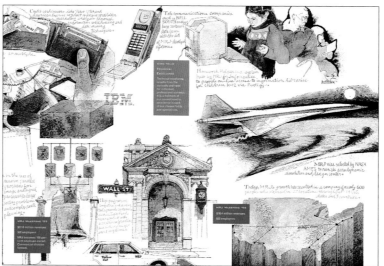

Design Firm:
Edward Walter Design,
Inc., New York, New York
Art Director/Designer:
Edward Walter
Illustrator:
Jack Unruh

Design & Printing

Nothing is more difficult than impressing one's peers, and proving that you can create a drop-dead design, or carefully execute someone else's drop-dead design, is the most difficult task set before the designer working on a promotion for distribution within the design industry. For a number of firms shown here, bigger is obviously better. Oversized booklets and brochures usually have no trouble catching the eye—but they had better maintain visual interest the whole way through. Grabbing the attention of passersby is obviously no problem for Mark Seliger, whose photographs have long brought in newsstand sales for *Rolling Stone*. But Miller/Kadanoff's brief was to bring in advertising rather than editorial assignments. Seliger's commentary is added to a 10" x 13" booklet displaying his celebrity photos, to emphasize his skill in conceptualizing unique approaches to people who have been endlessly photographed. Pierson Hawkins Inc. Advertising's 11" x 17" booklet for Brian Mark Photography takes a more abstract approach, designed around the themes of structure and form. Universal Press not only prints on a large scale—Les Jörgensen's fine-art photos are shown 10" x 17" in a calendar designed by Devine & Pearson Advertising—but the booklet is accompanied by one of the longest pencils you'll ever see, at 15" inches long. And few promotions are bigger than Keiler Design Group's 16" x 16" booklet for Lithographics, which allows the textures of Nick Pavloff's evocative photos to be scrutinized at close range.

Big can be beautiful, but small and exquisite also works—especially with a dose of humor. RJ Muna presents his photographic portfolio in a gorgeously printed

7 1/4" x 7 3/4" desk calendar, leavened with some self-deprecating "photo tips." Dorothy Nissen demonstrates her artistic and graphic skills in a 4 3/4" x 6" booklet titled "Confessions of My Inner Dog." Nissen sees Mars, the canine protagonist, as a symbol for her creativity, while also managing to satirize new-age literature. Copywriter Jill Spear looks back to an ancient device—the fable—to tell a story concluding with the moral, "Never hire a writer with an ordinary book." The 5 1/2" x 8 1/4" promotional booklet created by Esser Design to tell Spear's story is anything but ordinary, with hand-made endpapers and magical illustrations by John Nelson. A hand-bound, hand-glued, and hand-assembled folder by E.K. Weymouth Design and Karen Boyhen Illustration takes a fairly standard size, 9" x 11 3/4", but divides it into four envelopes, each of which houses an expressive collection of tiny items related to the four seasons, like scraps of lace, pieces of sheet music, dried leaves, and flower petals.

Humor in any form is also effective. A tin of peanuts packaged around a joke about working for "peanuts" serves as a self-promotional thank-you gift from Rodney Davidson, of DogStar Design & Illustration, and his rep, Terry Squire. Jon Flaming's brochure for Wilson Engraving utilizes John Craig's illustrations to skewer the past's vision of the future. Few things are more ripe for parody than award ceremonies, and Pierson Hawkins's call-for-entries brochure for the 1995-96 Denver Ad Show parodies stereotypical creative types and their self-important acceptance speeches, illustrated with caricatures by Chris Lensch that are very funny in themselves.

The portfolio booklet or brochure lends itself well to double duty as a promotion for both the client and the booklet's printer as with the piece designed by Pierson Hawkins Inc. Advertising for Brian Mark Photography (pp. 132–133). A portfolio containing works by illustrators represented by Arts Counsel Inc. gained coherence —and with costs kept down— through a conceptual theme of "Black and White" devised by Nestor.Stermole Visual Communications (pp. 134–135). A more personal approach to the portfolio is taken in books for photographers RJ Muna (which he designed himself; this spread) and Mark Seliger (whose book was done by Miller/Kadanoff; p. 130). Muna's desk calendar pokes fun at those who think the life of a photographer is all hobnobbing with celebrities. Seliger—whose work does involve hobnobbing with celebrities—entertains us with anecdotes about his famous subjects. The tug-of-war between imagination and budget is especially fierce for self-promotions—how do you achieve your wildest creative dreams without draining your own bank account? Dorothy Nissen kept costs down by working with a press still in its experimental stage (p. 128); Rodney Davidson of DogStar Design & Illustration collaborated with his rep on a gift tin of peanuts (p. 126); and E.K. Weymouth Design and Karen Boyhen Illustration made poetry from ordinary objects in a promotion that evokes the four seasons (p. 127).

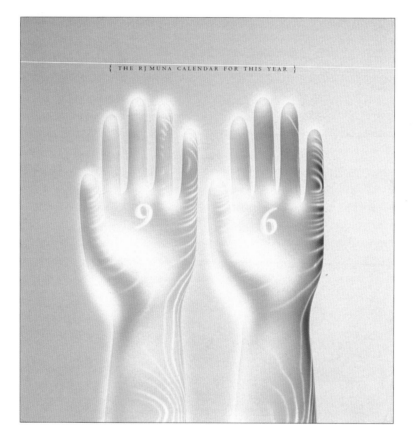

Art Director/ Photographer:
RJ Muna, San Francisco, California
Printer:
Craftsmen Printers

{ MARCH 11 TO MARCH 24 }

MO
11

TU
12

WE
13

TH
14

FR
15

SA
16

SU
17

MO
18

TU
19

WE
20

TH
21

FR
22

SA
23

SU
24

ST. PATRICK'S DAY

{ MARCH }

{ PHOTO TIP NUMBER 12 }

During a fashion shoot, it is not uncommon for models to undress and prep for the next shot in plain view. Seasoned pros are accustomed to this, but newcomers may not know how to react and become flustered. If you are approached by a naked fashion model, try to act nonchalant. Remember, they can smell fear.

{ APRIL }

{ JUMP }

{ SEPTEMBER 23 TO OCTOBER 6 }

MO
23

TU
24

WE
25

TH
26

FR
27

SA
28

SU
29

MO
30
YOM KIPPUR

TU
1

WE
2

TH
3

FR
4

SA
5

SU
6

{ SEPTEMBER }

{ PHOTO TIP NUMBER 77 }

The term "tool" is often used when referring to a Polaroid. This is a time-honored photographic terminology and it is considered bad form to snicker when you say it. You must brandish this term and others like it with unabashed confidence. It would be much the same as astronomers giggling every time they said "Uranus."

{ OCTOBER }

{ CROWDED FIELD }

To promote his photography, RJ Muna created this 7 1/4" x 7 3/4" wire-o bound desk calendar for 1996. Cover images of silvery, unearthly hands are wrapped around 50-pt. black Letramax sheets for added bulk and interest. Muna opens the book with an anecdote about being approached by a guy who wants to learn how to be a "Professional Photographer" because it's such a "cool" job, shooting those *Baywatch* babes. (Muna gives him the number of a mobile dog grooming truck, and tells him to ask for his pal, Pamela Anderson.) Images ranging from a color shot of a toy gas station to a black-and-white of a couple smooching atop a Harley-Davidson (parked, of course) alternate with lightly-tinted calendar pages that overlay faint tongue-in-cheek photography manual diagrams printed in white. The visuals are tied together with the use of punning titles (a man posed like an ancient Olympic athlete is called "Compact Discus") and Muna's "Photo Tips," such as what to do if you find you've been shooting without film in your camera: "simply say, 'This is so uncommon, I usually have big enough budgets to hire several assistants, and loading the camera would always be their job.' It is better than 'whoops.'"

When Rodney Davidson, of DogStar Design & Illustration, was asked by his rep, Terry Squire, to create a Christmas gift for their clients, he wanted to send something that was good to eat (peanuts) and good for a laugh (peanuts). The tins needed to be designed, illustrated, printed, and shipped within two weeks, as inexpensively as possible—thus demonstrating creativity within a budget. A 6"-square booklet tells the story of a peanut vendor whom Davidson remembers from his early career days. Davidson realized that he and the vendor (who promised his wares would "make yo' lips jump up and down") had something in common: "We were both working for peanuts." But now, thanks to his clients, he has "peanuts to spare." Boxes to hold the tins were hand-wrapped with hand-silk-screened paper; the booklets were laser-printed on black and brown Kraft paper and silver wrapping paper. The total cost came in at $11 per gift: $7 for the tin and packaging, $4 for shipping.

Design Firm:
DogStar Design & Illustration, Birmingham, Alabama
Art Director/Designer/ Illustrator/Copywriter:
Rodney Davidson

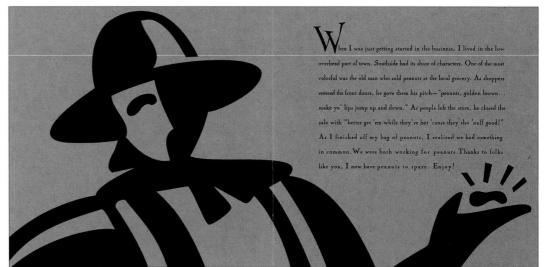

When I was just getting started in the business, I lived in the low overhead part of town. Southside had its share of characters. One of the most colorful was the old man who sold peanuts at the local grocery. As shoppers entered the front doors, he gave them his pitch—"peanuts, golden brown... make yo' lips jump up and down." As people left the store, he closed the sale with "better get 'em while they're hot 'cause they sho 'nuff good!" As I finished off my bag of peanuts, I realized we had something in common. We were both working for peanuts. Thanks to folks like you, I now have peanuts to spare. Enjoy!

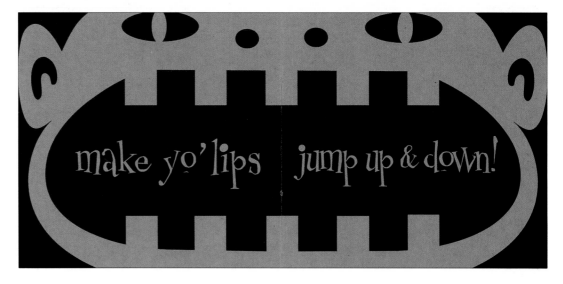

make yo' lips   jump up & down!

Eva Weymouth and Karen Boyhen report that this "Seasonal Sensations" brochure, promoting their respective design and illustration services, involved an enjoyable treasure hunt. To attract cookbook publishers, they wanted to create a piece combining recipes with items evocative of the different seasons, held within envelopes bound into a folder. Summer, for example, offers four recipes including cold cucumber soup with dill, a piece of lace, a rose petal, and a clipping from a map; Fall incorporates instructions for stuffed acorn squash, a leaf, a tea bag, and a button for a coat. Printed in 4-color process on Strathmore Grandee and Neenah Classic Linen, each 9" x 11 3/4" piece was hand-bound, hand-glued, and hand-assembled.

KAREN BOYHEN AND EVA WEYMOUTH

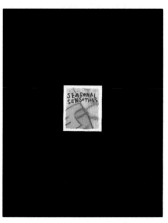

Design Firm:
E.K. Weymouth Design,
Riveron, Connecticut
Designer:
Eva Weymouth
Illustrator:
Karen Boyhen

DOROTHY NISSEN

Dorothy Nissen's offhand acrylic sketches of a friend's dog, Mars, suggested to her that the dog represented a part of herself—perhaps her creativity—and led to the creation of this self-promotional booklet, "Confessions of My Inner Dog." Mars's story, told through images painted over several months, thus comprises a narrative of how to relate to the imagination. Thrilled with the results achieved with the then-experimental Xeikon 4-color disk-driven printer, which allows for a great reduction in printing costs on very short runs, since no film or stripping is involved, Nissen designed the 56-page, 4 3/4" x 6" book to be an exact cut-out of two press sheets of 12" x 33". (Xeikon now suggests that this press functions best with smaller sheets, such as 9 1/2" x 12".) Background texture was made by scanning a piece of recycled paper with flecks and then increasing the magenta and adding noise to the scan, to suggest that it was handmade. Bauer Bodini was employed to provide a low-key, classical typographic context for the very direct style of the paintings, while the trendier Futura Condensed with dingbats between the letters of running heads evokes a mood of self-consciousness, in keeping with the deadpan portentousness of the text. Mars has since starred in four more books.

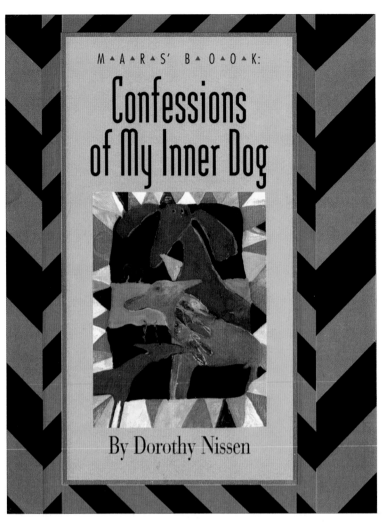

Designer/Illustrator/ Copywriter:
Dorothy Nissen, San Francisco, California

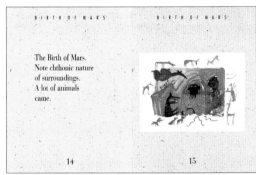

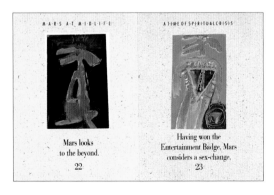

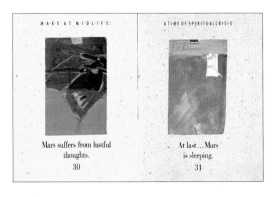

Design Firm:
Esser Design Inc.,
Phoenix, Arizona
Art Director:
Stephen Esser
Designer:
Jami Pomponi
Illustrator:
John Nelson
Copywriter:
Jill Spear

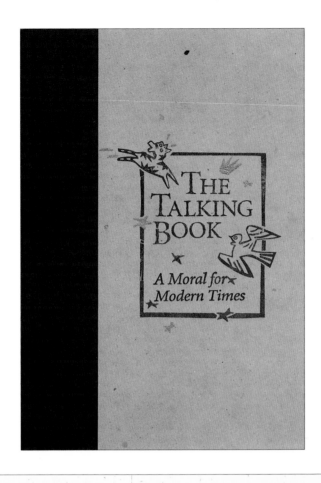

To interest design firms and advertising agencies in Jill Spear's copywriting services, Esser Design collaborated with the client on "The Talking Book: A Moral for Modern Times," the tale of an ancient Chinese leader who loses his province when he believes a scribe who claims to have invented a talking book. The moral of the story—"Never hire a writer with an ordinary book"—is amply embodied in this handcrafted piece, illustrated by John Nelson. The 5 1/2" x 8 1/4" cover, made of chip board and traditional bookbinding tape, was embellished with a rubber stamp using ink, gold embossing powder, and a heat gun. Handmade red paper with gold tinsel pressed into it serves as endpapers, while the text is printed on Proterra Flecks. The illustrations and custom typography were created in Adobe Illustrator. Spear paid for most of the book—design, printing, and illustration—by trading her copywriting services.

Then, one day, an advisor came to the prince with great news: A scribe had invented a talking book.

"They say the characters can speak, my prince. Even the pictures can move!" At last, Prince Chen was happy. "Send for this scribe and his book! Pay him whatever he wants, for no price is too great." When the advisor brought the scribe before the prince, the poor man was trembling. "Exalted prince, I beg your forgiveness," he said. "My wife is a boastful woman and made up stories to impress the neighbors. There's nothing magical about my book."

Moving pictures:
The prince imagines a book that can save his kingdom.

JILL SPEAR, COPYWRITER

MARK SELIGER, SHUTTERBUG

Mark Seliger, now chief photographer at *Rolling Stone*, hired Miller/Kadanoff to create a promotion piece that would attract more advertising-oriented assignments. While many of the photos shown in this brochure are familiar to *Rolling Stone* readers (and those who see the magazine on the newsstand), designer Paul Huber sought to capture Seliger's unique celebrity experiences in handwritten comments by the photographer. The 10" x 13" double-rivet-bound book, with covers in chipboard, has its title, "Mark Seliger, Shutterbug," printed on a pencil attached with a rubber band through the rivets in the binding. The pencils were "bitten" with pliers to add a level of realistic "angst." The design of the book was exchanged for a family portrait photograph, and the printing was traded for use as a printer's sample.

Michael Richards

Jeff Beck

John Lee Hooker

Mark Spitz

Metallica

Red Hot Chili Peppers

Design Firm:
Miller/Kadanoff,
San Francisco, California
Art Director/Designer:
Paul Huber
**Photographer/
Calligrapher:**
Mark Seliger
Editor:
Doris Mitsch

Design Firm:
Pierson Hawkins Inc.
Advertising, Denver,
Colorado
Art Director/Designer:
Brian Hawkins
Illustrator:
Chris Lensen
Copywriter:
Molly Worth

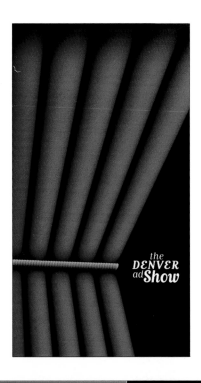

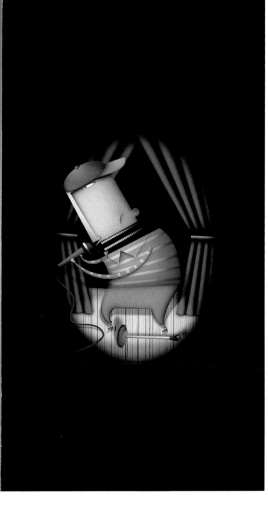

The theme of this call-for-entries brochure for the 1995-96 Denver Ad Show is the award acceptance speech. Each spread features an image of a creative "type," illustrated by Chris Lensch, and accompanied by his or her remarks once on stage. A blond-bobbed, pearl-wearing woman concludes, "give me advertising or give me death!" A backwards baseball-capped dude "thanks" his wife for failing to comfort him when he had pneumonia—otherwise, "I wouldn't have driven myself into the hospital where I was finally able to find the strength to finish the work." And a Birkenstocks-and-crystals woman admits that the award is meaningless "when you think of the hundreds and thousands of baby seals that are ruthlessly slaughtered every year," before announcing, "I'm moving to L.A. to work for Chiat Day." To impress the intended audience, Pierson Hawkins Inc. Advertising paid special attention to the quality of printing (by Lange Graphics on Island Mills/Dixon Paper Co. Bravo 100-lb. Dull Text and Cover), making sure that no "banding" occurred on the large gradations inside. Almost all costs for the 7" x 13" book were donated to benefit the non-profit Denver Advertising Federation.

DENVER ADVERTISING FEDERATION

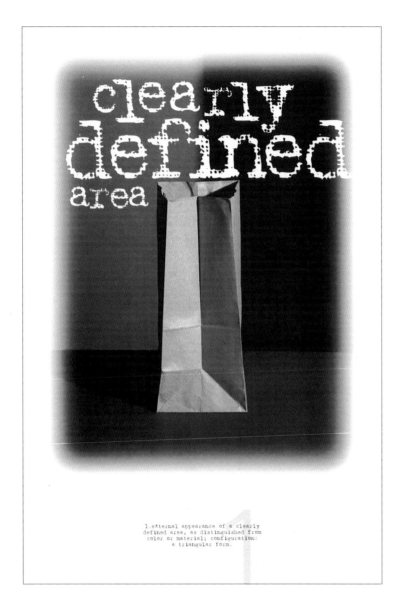

clearly
defined
area

1.external appearance of a clearly
defined area, as distinguished from
color or material; configuration:
a triangular form.

1

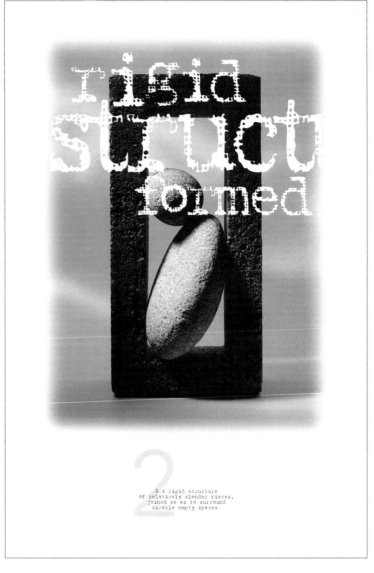

rigid
struct
formed

2.a rigid structure
of relatively slender pieces,
joined so as to surround
sizable empty spaces.

2

Design Firm:
Pierson Hawkins Inc.
Advertising, Denver,
Colorado
Art Director:
Brian Hawkins
Designer:
Janelle Aune
Photographer:
Brian Mark Photography
Copywriter:
David Knudten

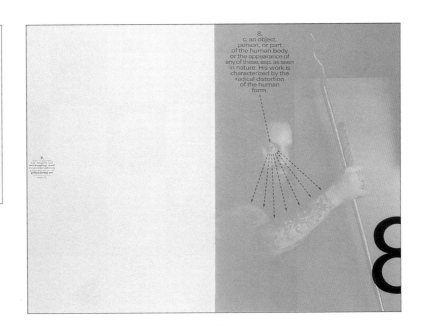

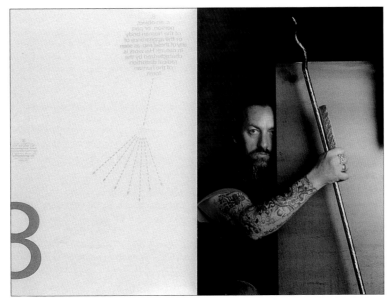

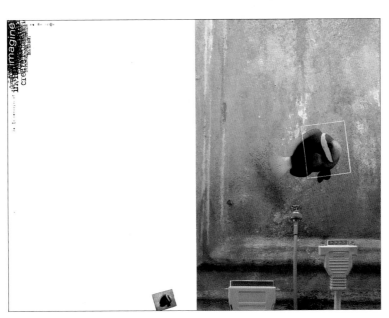

This promotion for Brian Mark Photography was designed by Pierson Hawkins Inc. Advertising to intrigue art directors in the Rocky Mountain region—and to win awards. (Obviously, it succeeded.) Finding a way to print the piece at a rate the client could afford was a more mundane challenge, solved by securing donated paper and arranging for a better price by designing the booklet to serve as a printer's sample as well. The 11" x 17" pages are printed on three stocks: uncoated and textured, glossy, and vellum. Images built upon Mark's photographs are organized around the themes of structure and form, whose dictionary definitions are matched to evocative visuals. Typewriter fonts, used "actual size" and blown up to near-disintegration, along with various sans-serifs, add to the generally "hip" feel of the piece.

BRIAN MARK PHOTOGRAPHY

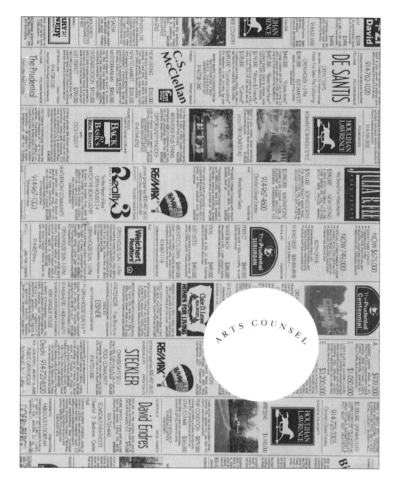

Illustrator: Claudia Pearson

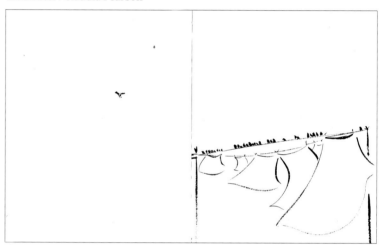

Illustrator: Sally Sturman

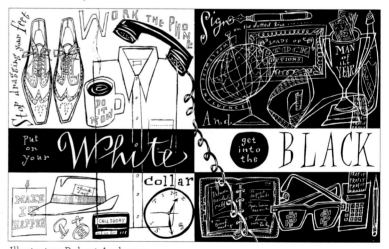

Illustrator: Robert Anderson

Calligrapher (left): Paul Shaw

Design Firm:
Nestor.Stermole Visual
Communications Group,
New York, New York
Art Director/Designer:
Rick Stermole

Illustrator: Robert Melee

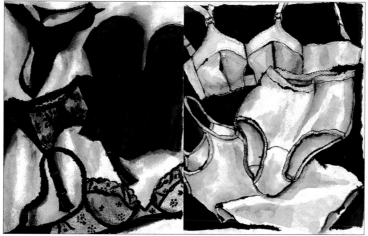

Illustrator: Pamela Kogen

Illustrator: Jeffrey Fulvimari

This "ultra low-tech" promotional brochure highlighting the illustrators represented by Arts Counsel, Inc. takes "Black and White" as its theme. The concept provides a consistent launching point for many diverse styles and makes it as easy as possible for potential clients to find appropriate artists—as it says on the mail return card, "It's as easy as black and white." Nestor.Stermole Visual Communications group assigned black-and-white objects or "situations" to the illustrators best suited to them. Individual leaves of Finch opaque white wove text paper were folded to accommodate 1-color offset printing (halftones and line art) on one side only, and the binding was hand-sewn. Covers were created from silkscreen-varnished pages of *The New York Times*, appropriate for these Big Apple–based artists' representatives. Mailed in a brown paper bag, and sealed with a sticker drawn to look like a keyhole, the 8" x 10" booklet has a tactile, gift-like quality, despite its low cost.

ARTS COUNSEL, INC.

It goes without saying that printing skills are the raison d'être for printer promotions. But how best to showcase a particular company's abilities? Devine & Pearson Advertising chose to go with the conceptual, almost fine-art photographs of Les Jörgensen in a vibrantly colored calendar for Universal Press (this spread). In contrast, highly naturalistic black-and-white photographs by Nick Pavloff lend visual cachet to the "Seeing" brochure for Lithographics devised by Keiler Design Group (p. 140). Vaughn Wedeen Creative combined stock and commissioned images from the Three Little Pigs to the Fab Four Beatles in a Cooper Press booklet (p. 138), assembling and manipulating the visuals in Photoshop, Quark XPress, and Adobe Illustrator. Jon Flaming (p. 141) combined his own high-energy logos with retro-futuristic collage illustrations by John Craig to emphasize Wilson Engraving's specialty—color. And David Lemley Design, in a calendar for Overlake Press (p. 139), and Sullivan Perkins, in a brochure for GTE Directories Printing (p. 142), both selected typographic solutions to show their clients to best advantage.

Design Firm:
Devine & Pearson Advertising, Quincy, Massachusetts
Creative Director:
John Pearson
Art Directors/Designers:
Clif Wong, Karen Genereux
Photographer:
Les Jörgensen
Production Manager:
Carly Olson

To showcase the 8-color press and straight-to-plate printing technology available from Universal Press, Devine & Pearson Advertising conceived this piece to function as "the Swiss Army knife of calendars," offering a variety of "tools" within it. Lavish photographs by Les Jörgensen of paint-encrusted tools of all sorts (described by the photographer as "sculpture that is integrated and pointed toward photography") face large (12 1/2" x 14") calendar pages. Jorgensen's tools correspond to the months they illustrate: a corkscrew for January, an abacus for April, and so on. A daily planner (3 1/2" x 6") is set within the die-cut calendar spreads. Tools are also incorporated on end-page spreads: diagrams for time zones, conversion tables, standard envelope sizes, and rules for both inches and points. The calendar and daily planner booklet are spiral-bound and held together by an oversized pencil inserted through the rings. The entire project was produced without film, using digital scanning, digital proofing, and digital plates.

UNIVERSAL PRESS

COOPER PRESS

This "One, Two, Color For You; Three, Four, Here's Some More" brochure by Vaughn Wedeen Creative highlights the pre-press and printing capabilities of Cooper Press. While the brochure had to showcase the client's specialty, 1- and 2-color printing, it also needed to assert 3- and 4-color options. A combination of stock and commissioned imagery makes these numerical points: a Dennis Darling duotone of twins, for instance, or a colorized Norm Bersuga shot of the Beatles. The size of the booklet (7" x 9") was determined by the client's press size, and printing was done on Mohawk Superfine Text two colors at a time, one signature per sheet. The book was saddle-stitched, and the Strathmore Grandee cover then perfect bound to the insides.

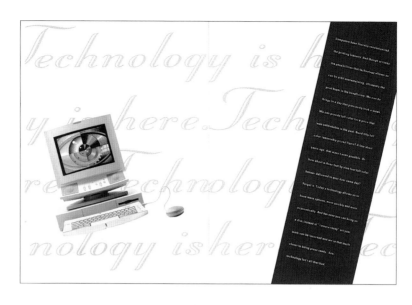

Design Firm:
Vaughn Wedeen
Creative, Albuquerque,
New Mexico
Art Director/Designer:
Dan Flynn
Copywriter:
Steve Wedeen
Photographer:
David Nofer
Illustrator:
Greg Tucker

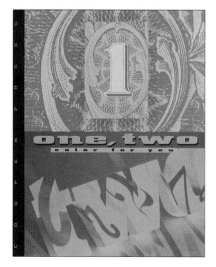

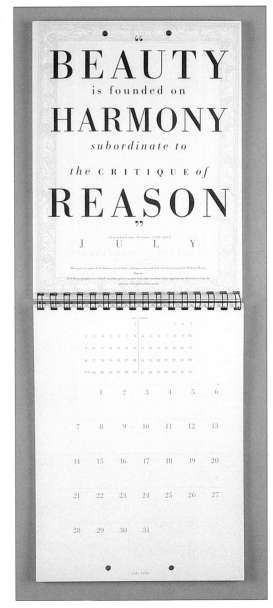

Design Firm:
David Lemley Design,
Seattle, Washington
Designer/Illustrator:
David Lemley

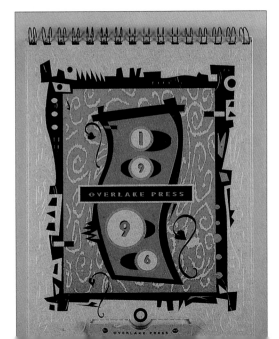

With this 1996 wall calendar for Overlake Press, David Lemley Design sought to create something that would not only stand out in the crowd of calendar freebies, but that would also establish the client as a business in close touch with the local design community and the skills required of designers. A theme of "Typography and Technique" carries this message, with the idea of communicating interesting information about typeface design from a classic context, and informing the audience how certain printing techniques were achieved within the calendar itself. The images are mainly typographic, and Lemley matched typefaces with months: For example, he says, "Aldo Novarese's rounded and sterile typeface, Eurostile, just felt like January, and crisp, classic, summery Bodoni seemed made for the month of July." Though he doesn't reject the new wave of type design, Lemley chose to employ typefaces that had influenced his personal design style. All but one were developed before 1960.

The two-prong paper fastener was requested by Overlake Press, which wanted something that would scar the wall only once, even though the calendar is fairly large (9" x 12").

The main goal of the "Seeing" booklet designed by Keiler Design Group for Lithographics was to look beyond the client's reputation as a small, 2-color printer to suggest that Lithographics is the place to go for the highest-quality jobs. To eliminate everyday clutter and entice the viewer, copy was limited to the booklet's endpages, with emphasis placed on the photography of Nick Pavloff. His original black-and-white prints were scanned as 4-color process. Specific areas of cyan or magenta were blocked out to give a cool tone to skies or a warm tone to the ground, which increases the feeling of depth of the overall image. Generously sized sheets (16" x 16") show off the photos to beautiful advantage. The front cover consists of a die-cut sheet folded over one of Pavloff's works.

Design Firm:
Keiler Design Group,
Farmington, Connecticut
Creative Directors:
Mike Scricco, Mel Maffei
Art Director/Designer:
Jeff Lin
Photographer:
Nicholas Pavloff
Copywriter:
Mel Maffei

Design Firm:
Jon Flaming Design,
Dallas, Texas
Art Director/Designer:
Jon Flaming
Illustrator:
John Craig

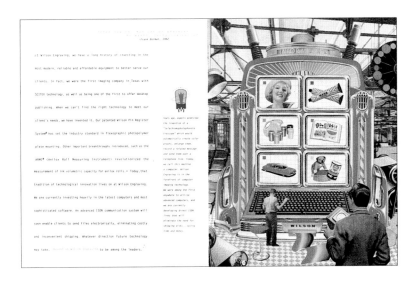

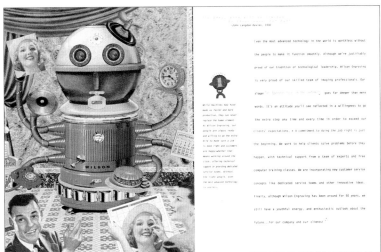

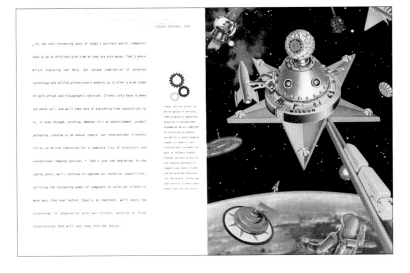

Wilson Engraving looked to Jon Flaming Design for this "To the Future" brochure, which stresses both Wilson's more than 50-year tradition and its vision for continued innovation. Flaming thought it would be fun to use imagery that captured what people in the 1930s thought the future would look like, and hired John Craig to create the collage-like illustrations. Bright, vibrant color—Wilson's specialty—was the main requirement, achieved through Craig's visuals and Flaming's signature logos representing concepts such as Wilson's position at the forefront of technology and its slogan, "an obsessive focus on the customer." The 8 1/2" x 11" brochure was printed in 4-color offset on Vicksburg Starwhite.

WILSON ENGRAVING

When GTE Directories Printing requested that employee testimonials play a significant role in its capabilities brochure, Sullivan Perkins decided to make the concept of quotation the brochure's main theme— "our directories have people talking" opens the text. A visual motif of quotation marks in combination with an oversized type treatment for the testimonials provides powerful visual and conceptual impact, making the quotes appear "larger than life." Transparent ink on Kraft-colored Gilbert Esse created an unusual overlap effect, and an opaque white ink was used to increase contrast. The art was done in Adobe Illustrator, with a "roughen" filter applied for a photocopy effect. The book measures 9" x 11 ½".

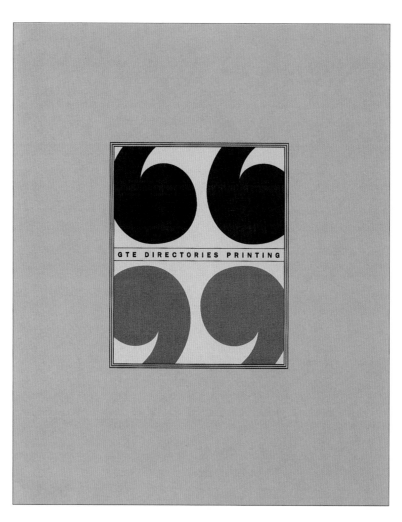

Design Firm:
Sullivan Perkins,
Dallas, Texas
Art Director:
Ron Sullivan
Designer:
Kelly Allen
Copywriters:
Chris Ault, Mark Perkins

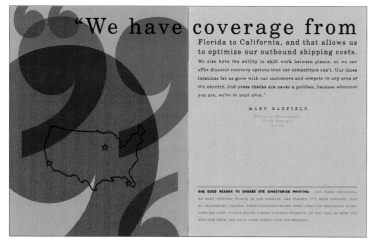

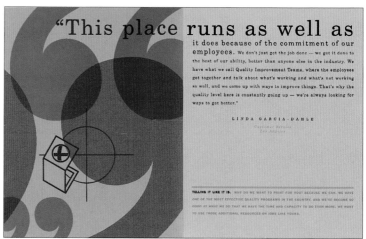

Paper Companies

Few design assignments are as research-intensive as the paper company promotion. Intimate familiarity with a company's papers and the printing processes best suited for them is just the beginning. Because demonstration of a paper's printing capabilities is the *raison d'être* of this type of promotion, a wide variety of imagery is usually required. This frequently involves countless hours of archival, stock, and illustrator and photographer source book research. And if that's not enough, historical and explanatory text is often added to make a piece more appealing as a reference tool or resource. In the end, of course, the project has great award-winning potential, but getting it done is a herculean creative and intellectual task.

The eight paper company promotions displayed in this section employ three thematic strategies: a narrow subject treated monographically; a narrow subject illustrated with a wide variety of visual examples; and a broad concept expressed through a broad variety of imagery. Design One's brochure for French paper firm Job Parilux, which lovingly showcases the glass-blown sculptures of Dale Chihuly, is an example of the first, monographic type. International Paper's "Innovation" brochure, by Cummings & Good, employs the specific theme of the company's innovations, but embodies it through a mix of illustration and photography. Pentagram Design's "Chair" brochure, to reintroduce Mohawk Superfine, features everything from Whistler's Mother to Herman Miller's Aeron chair to reinforce a concept of timelessness and versatility shared by the paper and the piece of furniture.

Brochures for Hopper Papers and Weyerhaeuser treat the same type of theme—"God Bless America"—through different strategies. The "Borders" brochure by Wages Design for Hopper looks at the boundaries separating the U.S. from Canada and Mexico, linking them through the photographs of Doug Baartman. "Route 66" provides a theme of America's creative spirit in a Pentagram-designed brochure for Weyerhaeuser. Vintage postcards, travel decals, motel signs, and cars; a painting of the Grand Canyon, photographs of Woody Guthrie and John Steinbeck, a photograph by Dorothea Lange; and a text written with the assistance of Route 66 historian Michael Wallis are among the elements combined to highlight the capabilities of Cougar Opaque.

Most ambitious of all are the three brochures that tackle broad concepts in every imaginable permutation; it is perhaps significant that all three were created by Pentagram. A booklet titled "Tools of the Trade #2: Photography on Starwhite Vicksburg" was commissioned by Simpson Paper Company to feature the rich variety available through the medium and through their line. A three-booklet "Options" promotion for Mohawk's new line that "feels like uncoated paper but prints like nothing you've ever seen" uses images of everything from 17 different pairs of scissors to a fashion model transformed with wigs and contacts to make the point that Americans love options. Finally, "Rethinking Design II: The Future of Print" takes a more intellectual approach, presenting the work of top designers, writers, and illustrators in a text-heavy piece to reinforce the importance of ink on paper. From the evidence at hand—the sensuous tactility of these three pieces—the future of print is strong indeed.

Design Firm:
Pentagram Design,
New York, New York
Art Director:
Michael Bierut
Designer:
Esther Bridavsky

CHAIR AS HISTORY *on* ARCHIVAL
MOHAWK SUPERFINE

MANKIND HAS ALWAYS YEARNED
for a comfy spot to sit, but during much
of our species' evolution, good seating
has been hard to find. Prehistoric man sat
on rocks, later to be substituted by
stumps, more aesthetically appealing, but
just as unyielding. Today's citizen
has his or her choice of recliners, from
a modern butterfly construction to
an ergonomically correct office chair.
While our seating arrangements
evolved rapidly, we have grown very
slowly: man's measurements have varied
by mere inches during the past 500,000
years, but his chair has made great leaps.

ORIGINAL SUPERFINE
AND INTRODUCING
NEW ULTRAWHITE SUPERFINE

c h a i r

CHAIR AS FINE ART *on* BRILLIANT
MOHAWK SUPERFINE

For Mohawk Paper Mills' relaunch of their flagship paper line, Pentagram developed this 9" x 11 3/4" brochure. A theme of "Chairs" represents the timelessness and versatility of Mohawk Superfine. In order to capture the fine qualities of this stock, as well as significant product enhancements including a new bright white color and a range of recycled papers, images of chairs are depicted using a variety of printing and production techniques. For example, a picture of a hypnotized woman suspended between two chairs is printed on the left page of the spread in PMS 876 and Black duotone on Softwhite 80 Text Smooth Finish, and on the right page in the same inks but on Softwhite 100 Text Eggshell Finish. On another page, design student Brendán Murphey's sketches and prototype for a new Mobility Impaired Symbol demonstrate Black foilstamp, registered emboss on White 65 Cover Smooth finish.

CHAIR AS REST OR WORRY-FREE
MOHAWK SUPERFINE

MAKE FUN OF IT IF YOU WILL: the overstuffed reclining chair is America's best-selling piece of furniture. These metaphors for sloth have been sold since before the depression, and once TV was invented, volume soared. Models are offered for one or side-by-side couples. Are these chairs classy? No. Irresistible? Yes. For all the jokes about lost change, pulverized chips and beer stains, women buy some 65% of them. Rule of thumb: the bigger the TV, the more reclining chairs. One customer bought two 14-foot by four-foot recliner sectionals to form a horseshoe. "I always know where my kids are," he says.

Chair today...

gone tomorrow

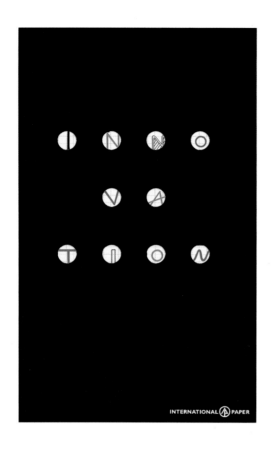

INTERNATIONAL ▲ PAPER

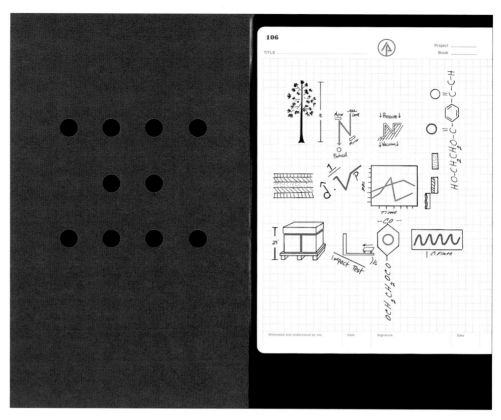

TITLE _____   Project _____
Book _____

Witnessed and understood by me.   Date   Signature   Date

Wild Idea

Beverage companies had a problem. Under pressure from environmentalists and wildlife advocates, states were proposing to ban the plastic rings that linked six-packs.

International Paper had a solution. A team of experts that included packaging designers and engineers, production specialists and analytical chemists refined a design for a biodegradable, recyclable paperboard beverage carrier that poses no risk to fish or waterfowl. And it actually outperforms plastic in shake tests.

What's more, this new Trilex™ carrier turns out to have other advantages. Its rigidity virtually eliminates the jiggling that often damages plastic-yoked cans and bottles, and improves stackability in trucks, stores and warehouses. The paperboard also provides a printable surface for logos, graphics or promotional copy — a big plus in the high-stakes retail beverage industry.

Major wildlife and environmental groups have endorsed the new product. And beverage companies have adopted it for multipacked bottles as well as for cans.

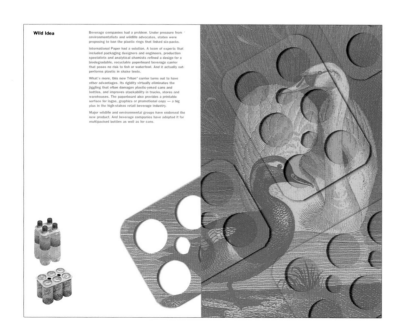

Breaking the Mold

What happens when you apply papermaking technology to polyethylene? For starters, a remarkable new label material called Polyweave? It solves some sticky problems with plastic bottles.

Instead of being glued, Polyweave labels are applied "in mold" so that they actually become part of the bottle's structure. There's no need to separate these labels before regrinding the plastic bottles, and no sticky glue residues to contaminate the recycling process.

Polyweave also eliminates the blistering associated with film labels because it doesn't trap air between the label and bottle. Yet this first synthetic substrate produced with papermaking techniques can be printed on an offset press — just like paper — for eye-catching graphic appeal.

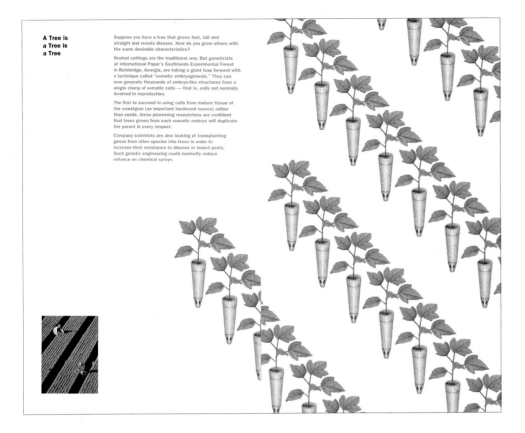

**A Tree is
a Tree is
a Tree**

Suppose you have a tree that grows fast, tall and straight and resists disease. How do you grow others with the same desirable characteristics?

Rooted cuttings are the traditional way. But geneticists at International Paper's Southlands Experimental Forest in Bainbridge, Georgia, are taking a giant leap forward with a technique called "somatic embryogenesis." They can now generate thousands of embryo-like structures from a single clump of somatic cells — that is, cells not normally involved in reproduction.

The first to succeed in using cells from mature tissue of the sweetgum (an important hardwood source) rather than seeds, these pioneering researchers are confident that trees grown from each somatic embryo will duplicate the parent in every respect.

Company scientists are also looking at transplanting genes from other species into trees in order to increase their resistance to disease or insect pests. Such genetic engineering could markedly reduce reliance on chemical sprays.

Design Firm:
Cummings & Good,
Chester, Connecticut
Designer:
Peter Good
Illustrator:
Janet Cummings Good
Photographer:
Steve Kahn

Cummings & Good created this "Innovation" brochure to dramatically express the spirit of innovation at International Paper by showcasing its recent developments, like Riverdale 16, the world's biggest, fastest paper machine. A cover design involving die-cut circles which isolate letters from a drawing on the page beneath suggests that innovation can be elusive, and can be revealed by a change in context. Spreads combine a variety of stock images, commissioned photography, and illustrations, manipulated in Photoshop and Scitex Blaze. (International Paper acquired an interest in Scitex in 1992.) The 8 $^{1}/_{2}$" x 14" wire-o bound booklet is printed on Ikonofix Matt 100-lb. Text, with Everest folding carton board, 24 point.

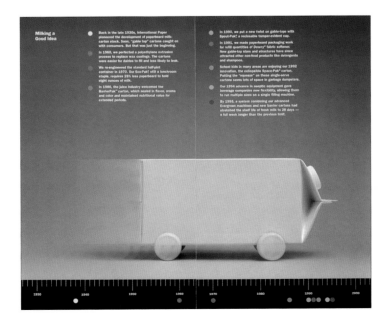

Milking a
Good Idea

Back in the late 1930s, International Paper pioneered the development of paperboard milk-carton stock. Soon, "gable top" cartons caught on with consumers. But that was just the beginning.

In 1960, we perfected a polyethylene extrusion process to replace wax coatings. The cartons were easier for dairies to fill and less likely to leak.

We re-engineered the standard half-pint container in 1970. Our Eco-Pak® still a lunchroom staple, requires 25% less paperboard to hold eight ounces of milk.

In 1986, the juice industry welcomed the BarrierPak® carton, which sealed in flavor, aroma and color and maintained nutritional value for extended periods.

In 1990, we put a new twist on gable-tops with Spout-Pak,® a reclosable tamper-evident cap.

In 1991, we made paperboard packaging work for refill quantities of Downy® fabric softener. New gable-top sizes and structures have since attracted other non-food products like detergents and shampoos.

School kids in many areas are enjoying our 1992 innovation, the collapsible Space-Pak® carton. Putting the "squeeze" on these single-serve cartons saves lots of space in garbage dumpsters.

Our 1994 advance in aseptic equipment gave beverage companies new flexibility, allowing them to run multiple sizes on a single filling machine.

By 1995, a system combining our advanced Evergreen machines and new barrier cartons had stretched the shelf life of fresh milk to 28 days — a full week longer than the previous limit.

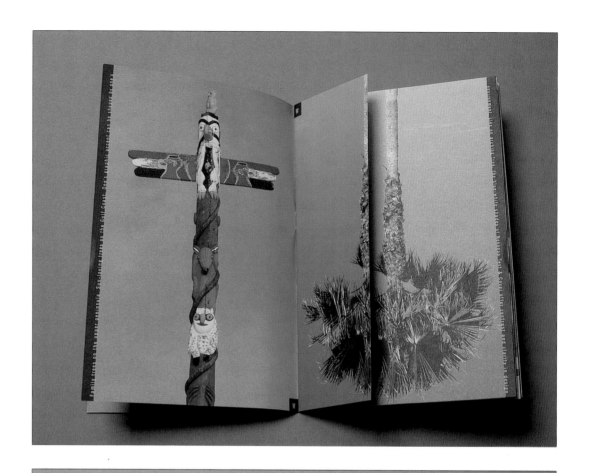

Design Firm:
Wages Design,
Atlanta, Georgia
Art Directors:
Ted Fabella, Bob Wages
Designer:
Ted Fabella
Photographer:
Doug Baartman
Copywriter:
Matthew Porter

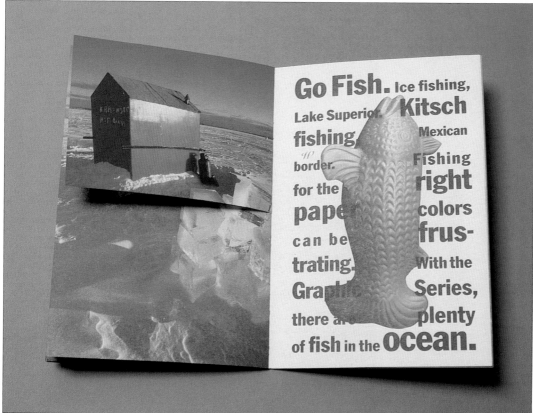

Hopper Papers assigned Wages Design to create a promotional series that would be functional rather than flashy. To distinguish these pieces from the over-sized promotions distributed by many competitors, a small (6" x 9") size was chosen. This example, printed on Nekoosa Text and Cover, is sized to fit in a binder with other Hopper Papers promotions. The "Borders" series takes as its theme the boundaries that define the U.S. and separate it from its northern and southern neighbors, Canada and Mexico. The photographer, Doug Baartman, was sent out with the mission of capturing images indigenous to each of the border areas: a hot Texas porch, Niagara Falls on a winter day. Certain pairings and juxtapositions emerged as stories. A visual comparison of these borders echoes the brochure's business theme, a comparison of waterless and conventional printing processes.

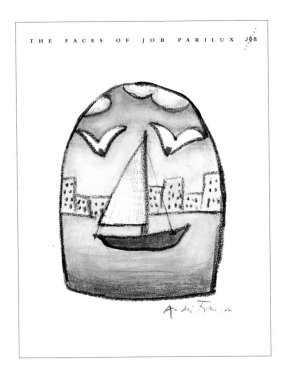

THE FACES OF JOB PARILUX J⬦B

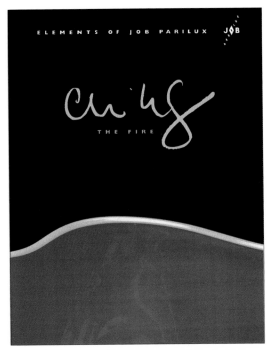

ELEMENTS OF JOB PARILUX J⬦B

THE FIRE

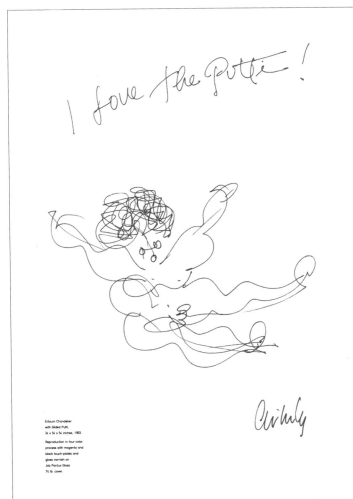

I love the Putti!

Erbium Chandelier
with Gilded Putti,
34 x 54 x 54 inches, 1993.

Reproduction in four-color
process with magenta and
black touch-plates and
gloss varnish on
Job Parilux Gloss
74 lb. cover.

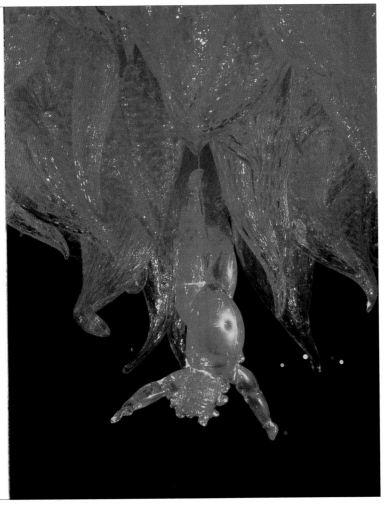

Design Firm:
Design One,
San Francisco, California
Art Directors:
Jacqueline Ghosin, James
Fash, Franz Platte
Designers:
Jacqueline Ghosin, James
Fash, Franz Platte, Alisa
Rudloff, Chris Peterson,
Gayle Marsh

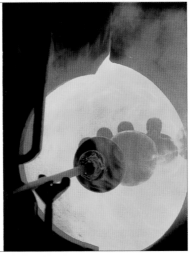

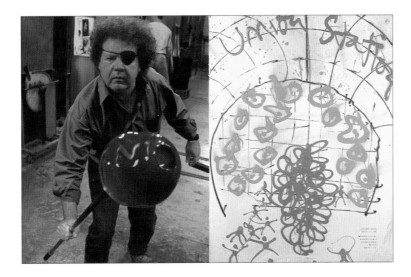

Job Parilux, in Toulouse, France, manufactures ultra-premium coated art papers. When the company wanted to introduce its products to the U.S., it looked to Design One for brochures that would attract clients such as art-book publishers and the designers of high-end annual reports. The designers sought to capitalize on Job Parilux's long history of association with the arts in France by positioning the company as an art patron in the U.S. Extraordinary glass blower Dale Chihuly provided transparencies from his archives, augmented with handwritten comments about his work. Images of the richly colored glass sculptures were printed as large and as dynamically cropped as possible to intimately engage the viewer. The use of geometric screening in the printing process allowed for much higher ink densities than conventional screening, and also provided better handling of subtle color curves. Red, green, and black touchplates were also employed for the 9" x 12" booklet. Another piece for the series illustrates the theme of "exceptional faces," with a cover design by André François.

JOB PARILUX

Design Firm:
Sibley/Peteet Design,
Dallas, Texas
Art Director:
Don Sibley
Photographer:
Dick Patrick

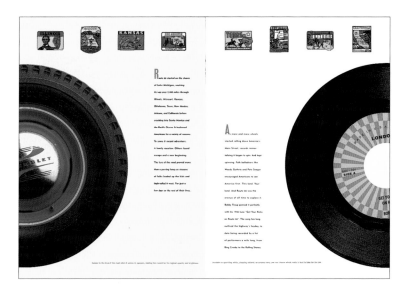

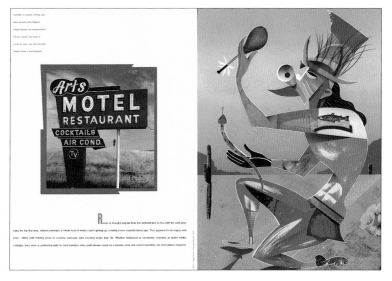

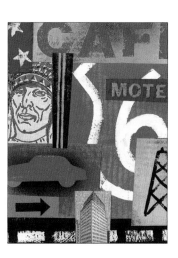

"Route 66" is the third in a series of "American Artifacts" brochures created by Sibley/Peteet Design for Weyerhaeuser Paper in celebration of America's creative spirit. Archival images from museums and individual collectors, stock photos, and specifically commissioned visuals depicting the historical American highway were combined in the hope that those who received the brochure would be enticed to add it to their permanent reference materials. A die-cut cover (9" x 12 1/2") holds an accordion-fold series of five vintage postcard reproductions, and additional postcards are found on a gatefold back cover. Inside the book, an accordion-fold pullout depicts Cadillac Ranch, an infamous Texas attraction. The brochure was printed on Weyerhaeuser Cougar Opaque and Cougar Natural Opaque using the latest in waterless technology, with 300-line conventional screens.

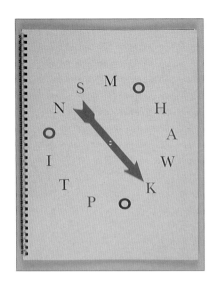

Design Firm:
Pentagram Design,
New York, New York
Art Director:
Michael Bierut
Designer:
Emily Hayes

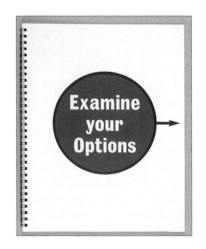

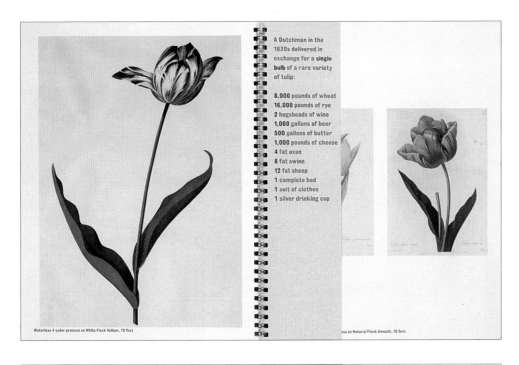

A Dutchman in the 1630s delivered in exchange for a **single bulb** of a rare variety of tulip:

8,000 pounds of wheat
16,000 pounds of rye
2 hogsheads of wine
1,000 gallons of beer
500 gallons of butter
1,000 pounds of cheese
4 fat oxen
8 fat swine
12 fat sheep
1 complete bed
1 suit of clothes
1 silver drinking cup

Waterless 4-color process on White Fleck Vellum, 70 Text

...ss on Natural Fleck Smooth, 70 Text

1 = Heife-Weizen
Refreshing, light body and hops, high effervescence, fruitiness from a high percentage of wheat, flavor and aroma suggest bananas and cloves. Serve unfiltered, the cloudiness comes from yeast.

2 = Porter
Rich, almost black ale, medium maltiness and body, fruity, dry, low hoppiness. Favorite of London's railroad porters and George Washington.

3 = India Pale Ale
Fruity, extremely hoppy, higher alcohol, medium maltiness. Developed to withstand the sea voyage from Britain to India.

4 = American Amber Ale
Copper, medium body, low to medium maltiness, citrussy, high hop flavor, aroma and bitterness. Use of Pacific Northwest hops essential.

4-color process with Geometric DOT™ screening on Natural Heather Vellum, 70 Text

...eening on White Fleck Vellum, 80 Cover

Microbrews courtesy of Flying Fish

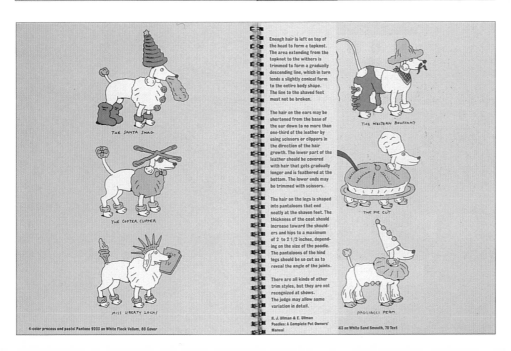

Enough hair is left on top of the head to form a topknot. The area extending from the topknot to the withers is trimmed to form a gradually descending line, which in turn lends a slightly conical form to the entire body shape. The line to the shaved feet must not be broken.

The hair on the ears may be shortened from the base of the ear down to no more than one-third of the leather by using scissors or clippers in the direction of the hair growth. The lower part of the leather should be covered with hair that gets gradually longer and is feathered at the bottom. The lower ends may be trimmed with scissors.

The hair on the legs is shaped into pantaloons that end neatly at the shaven feet. The thickness of the coat should increase toward the shoulders and hips to a maximum of 2 to 2 1/2 inches, depending on the size of the poodle. The pantaloons of the hind legs should be so cut as to reveal the angle of the joints.

There are all kinds of other trim styles, but they are not recognized at shows. The judge may allow some variation in detail.

H. J. Ullman & E. Ullman
Poodles: A Complete Pet Owners' Manual

THE SANTA SHAG

THE COPTER CLIPPER

MISS LIBERTY LOCKS

THE WESTERN BOUFFANT

THE PIE CUT

PAGLIACCI PERM

4-color process and pastel Pantone 9205 on White Fleck Vellum, 80 Cover

...63 on White Sand Smooth, 70 Text

In 1995, Mohawk Paper Mills invented a new paper process to make a stock that looks and feels like uncoated, but offers the printability and ink holdout of coated. Called Mohawk Options, the paper is available in a wide range of colors and finishes; plain, speckled, and fibered; and virgin and recycled. Pentagram Design developed this three-booklet promotional package on the theme of "Options." The main piece, measuring 9" x 12", illustrates how people exercise their options in life: customizing their mailboxes, changing their hair and eye color, choosing between a porter and an India pale ale microbrewed beer. Each example was depicted by a different artist, from 17th-century tulip painter Georg Dionysius Ehret to New York photographers Davies and Starr and designer Seymour Chwast. Short sheets and gatefolds add interest. An 8 1/2" x 11" book featuring the same photo of model Kara Underwood printed on various stocks with different processes and a 5 1/2" x 9" swatchbook accompany the main "Options" piece.

MOHAWK PAPER MILLS

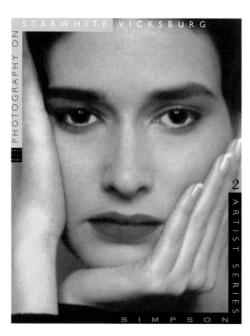
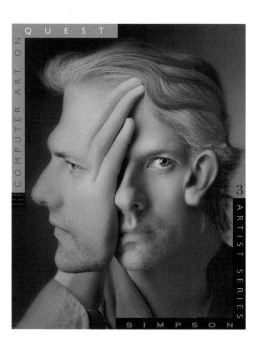

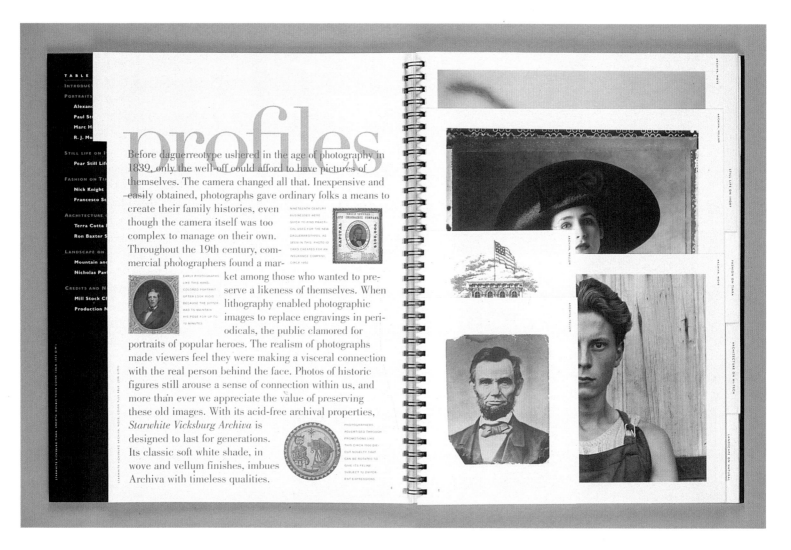

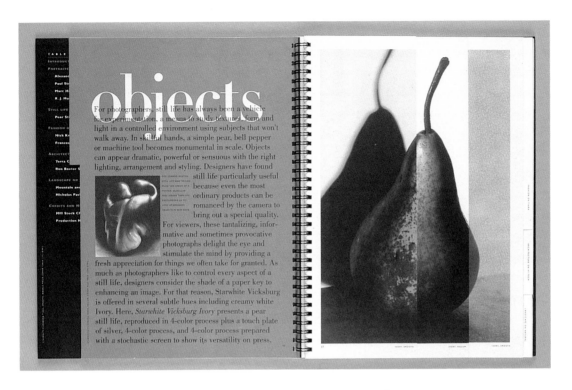

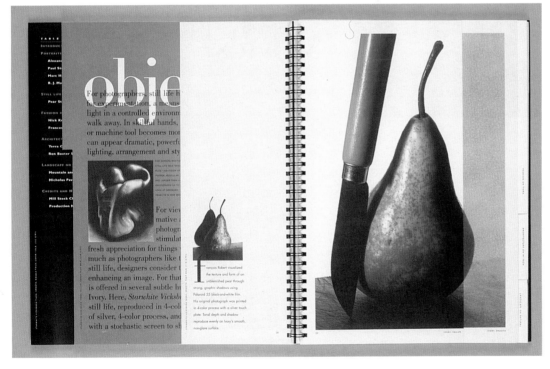

Simpson Paper Company asked Pentagram to create "Tools of the Trade #2: Photography on Starwhite Vicksburg," a 9" x 12" booklet reflecting the rich potential of photography and design. At the same time, the piece needed to clarify a complex line of high-quality uncoated paper. To organize the book, Pentagram defined categories of photography and matched them to types of paper: for example, "Still Life on Ivory" and "Fashion on Tiara." Each section includes a variety of images printed on different sizes and finishes, such as an Alexander Gardner's photograph of Lincoln on Archiva, Vellum; a young farmer by Paul Strand on Archiva, Wove; and an image of a woman in a hat from a personal portrait project by contemporary photographer Marc Hauser on Archiva, Vellum. Other pieces in the series include "#1: Drawing on Evergreen" and "#3: Computer Art on Quest." The success of the reproductions required over 36 exhausting press proofs.

Design Firm:
Pentagram Design, New York, New York
Art Directors:
Woody Pirtle, John Klotnia
Designers:
John Klotnia, Ivette Montes de Oca

"Rethinking Design II: The Future of Print" is the second in a series of occasional publications from Mohawk that examines design questions. Pentagram provided a vision for this 9 ¹/₂" x 12 ¹/₄" piece, published in March 1995, which serves to advance Mohawk's profile within the design industry and demonstrates the virtues of Mohawk's papers. Contributions from well-known figures in the design field such as writer Janet Abrams, illustrator Stephen Kroninger, and designer Edward Fella benefit from a vibrantly-colored layout by Michael Bierut and Emily Hayes of Pentagram. The cover was printed on Mohawk Vellum 65-lb. Cover Jute and the interior text on Mohawk Satin 80-lb. Text Cool White Recycled; images were scanned and output using a 175-line Scitex GeometricDOT screen.

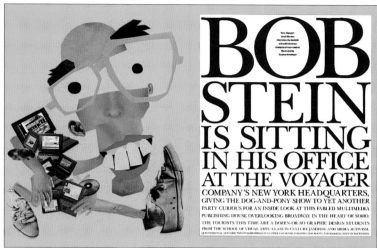

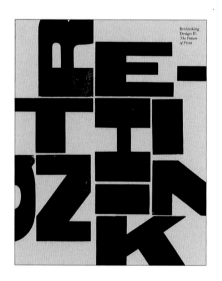

Design Firm:
Pentagram Design,
New York, New York
Art Director:
Michael Bierut
Designers:
Emily Hayes, Michael
Bierut

TOURISM AND TRAVEL

Though one might expect booklets and brochures promoting local businesses, services, and attractions to be built around documentary photographs, only one of the seven pieces shown here employs the camera's vision as its main graphic device. Even that booklet, the Park People's Harris County Tree Registry, takes a fine-art turn, with photographs of the Houston area's largest and most distinguished trees shown in color photos, and black-and-white shots colorized for an antique effect. Savage Design Group adds to the book's natural appeal by using handmade paper incorporating small leaves for fly sheets.

The other six pieces in this section eschew photo-graphic realism in favor of a stylized, limited-color appearance, or a highly personal, artistic presentation. Budget and format limitations meant that Scott Johnson Design needed to make the most of black, white, and PMS 1205 palette for brochures commissioned by the Rockford Area Convention & Visitors Bureau. Johnson succeeded with diverting symbols that make the most of two-color printing through positive/negative reversals. Royal, in a "Memphis by the Numbers: Facts and Figures You Can Use" brochure for the Bureau of Business and Economic Research of the University of Memphis, devised an unusual format (3 1/2" x 12") and an embossed cover in French Paper Dur-o-Tone bound with box staples to produce something unexpected in the world of business statistics.

John Sayles Design's "Warehouse Greater Des Moines" brochure also explores new territory in the world of business, with a piece formed from cardboard, wingnuts, manila tag, and packaging stickers. Though created from the stuff of warehouses, this piece is like nothing to have passed through the hands of those who decide where to locate a company's shipping hub.

The Charlotte Inn, on Martha's Vineyard in Massachusetts, aims to make guests feel at home in an atmosphere of Edwardian elegance. A brochure by Kolodny & Rentschler evokes another age through Marilyn Caldwell's watercolors, which detail rooms throughout the inn. Still-lifes such as a bedside lamp and book, or portraits of Andrew and Morgan, the resident dogs, with cups and saucers at their feet, suggest that the Charlotte Inn does indeed "exude an unpretentious sense of class and refinement," as one reviewer is quoted. When the Four Seasons Hotel in Washington, D.C., hosted the installation of Raymond Mason's 10'-long and 4'-deep sculpture on the theme of the last day of the Les Halles Market in Paris, Wood Design produced a commemorative brochure in the form of the artist's sketchbook. Mike McConnell literally reproduced his sketchbook of line drawings recorded during a visit to the Jamaica Inn in Ocho Rios. While McConnell's comments are quite tiny, they reward the attentive reader, especially the story of his response to a Jamaican air traffic controller strike.

Of the four pieces in this section devoted to promoting local businesses, services, and attractions, only one utilizes photographs as its main visual device. The other three use bold and simple graphics in limited colors to make their points. To encourage businesses to locate warehouses in the travel and transportation hub of Des Moines, Iowa, Sayles Design developed a "Warehouse Greater Des Moines" booklet (this spread) from materials familiar to warehouse users: cardboard, wingnuts, and stickers and seals reading "Fragile" or "Rush." The piece was commissioned by the Greater Des Moines Chamber of Commerce. Scott Johnson Design's "Hotel Guide" and "Things to Do Guide" for the Rockford (Illinois) Area Convention & Visitors Bureau employ lively positive/negative symbols and type treatments to add interest to the standard 8 1/2" x 11" three-fold brochure format (p. 162). "Memphis By the Numbers: Facts and Figures You Can Use," designed by Royal for the Bureau of Business and Economic Research of the University of Memphis, makes a virtue of an unusual format, measuring 12" x 3 1/2" (p. 163). In contrast to these stylized pieces, The Harris County Tree Registry, created by Savage Design Group for the Park People, attracts readers (and buyers) with fine-art photographs of the largest and most distinguished trees in the Houston region of Texas (p. 164–165).

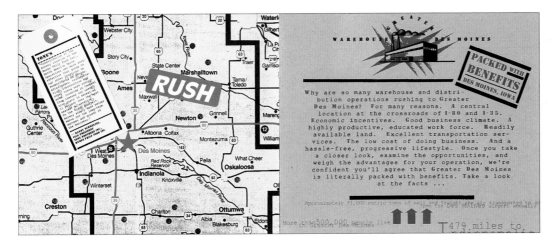

Design Firm:
Sayles Graphic Design,
Inc., Des Moines, Iowa
**Art Director/Designer/
Illustrator:**
John Sayles

To promote Des Moines as a transportation and travel hub, the Greater Des Moines Chamber of commerce hired Sayles Graphic Design to produce this "Warehouse" promotion. In creating the booklet, Sayles utilized materials familiar to warehouse personnel, such as corrugated cardboard (for covers), wingnuts (for the binding), and stickers, seals, and shipping tags (for visual effect). The interior pages are printed in two colors with Sayles's hand-rendered illustrations and grainy photographs of the city and its transportation alternatives on manila tag and cover weight Curtis Tuscan Terra Flax. No art was produced on the computer. Shipping tags are printed with testimonials from businesses satisfied with Des Moines-area locations. Stencil typography developed by Sayles is screenprinted on the 13" x 9" cover, accented by a die-cut. A perforated reply card is included, and the mailer is held closed with "Do Not Inventory" box tape.

Scott Johnson Design created these two brochures, "Hotel Guide" and "Things To Do Guide," for the Rockford Area Convention & Visitors Bureau in Illinois, along with a calendar of events. The Bureau specified that the pieces should fit existing displays and #10 envelopes with an 8 ¹/₂" x 11" three-fold format, and could only be printed in two colors. Johnson chose black and PMS 1205. Because displays sometimes cover the bottom half of the brochure, a simple positive/negative bar at top provides the necessary information and allows for typographic flexibility and unity. The positive/negative effect continues through lively line art and symbols which were hand-drawn and then scanned in as a template to Illustrator, where they were refined, and imported into Quark XPress. For display statewide, 75,000 copies of "Things To Do" were printed, along with 25,000 copies of the hotel brochure.

Design Firm:
Scott Johnson Design, Rockford, Illinois
Art Director/Designer:
Scott Johnson

Design Firm:
Royal,
Memphis, Tennessee
Art Director/Designer/
Illustrator:
Royal
Printer:
Advantage Printing

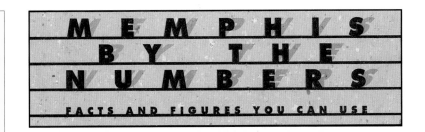

The Bureau of Business and Economic Research of the University of Memphis, Tennessee, turned to Royal for the design of a brochure that would present BBER and the information it provides in a fun format. The resulting piece, "Memphis By the Numbers: Facts and Figures You Can Use," succeeds in communicating to the business community that BBER's facts about the city can improve their bottom line. Because Royal's budget was limited, the interior of the book was kept to two colors and focus placed on the unusually sized cover (12" x 3 1/2"), with its embossed lettering, box staples, and French Paper Dur-o-Tone Packing Carton stock. Stock illustrations from a Letrafont disk add interest to the interior pages, along with amusing facts such as "Number of entrants in Schering-Plough's 'Little Miss Coppertone' Lookalike Contest in 1993: More than 100,000." More serious information, such as Memphis Debit/Credit and statistics on population, growth, and work force, is presented in appealing charts and graphs.

BBER, UNIVERSITY OF MEMPHIS

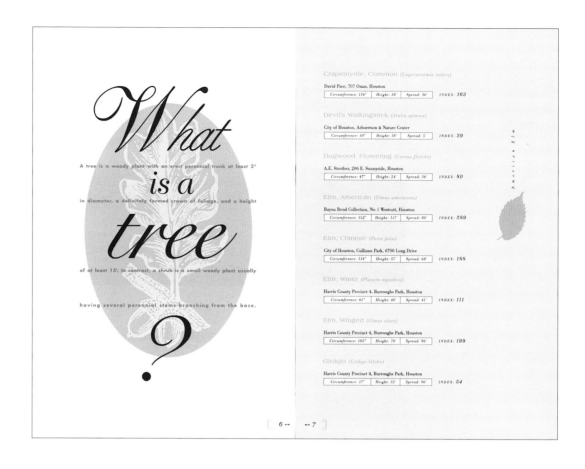

What is a tree?

A tree is a woody plant with an erect perennial trunk at least 3" in diameter, a definitely formed crown of foliage, and a height of at least 13'. In contrast, a shrub is a small woody plant usually having several perennial stems branching from the base.

Crapemyrtle, Common *(Lagerstroemia indica)*
David Pace, 707 Omar, Houston

| Circumference: 116" | Height: 38' | Spread: 36' | INDEX: 163 |

Devil's Walkingstick *(Aralia spinosa)*
City of Houston, Arboretum & Nature Center

| Circumference: 10" | Height: 18' | Spread: 5' | INDEX: 29 |

Dogwood, Flowering *(Cornus florida)*
A.E. Strother, 206 E. Sunnyside, Houston

| Circumference: 47" | Height: 24' | Spread: 36' | INDEX: 80 |

Elm, American *(Ulmus americana)*
Bayou Bend Collection, No. 1 Westcott, Houston

| Circumference: 152" | Height: 117' | Spread: 80' | INDEX: 289 |

Elm, Chinese *(Parvi folia)*
City of Houston, Cullinan Park, 6700 Long Drive

| Circumference: 114" | Height: 57' | Spread: 68' | INDEX: 188 |

Elm, Water *(Planera aquatica)*
Harris County Precinct 4, Burroughs Park, Houston

| Circumference: 61" | Height: 40' | Spread: 41' | INDEX: 111 |

Elm, Winged *(Ulmus alata)*
Harris County Precinct 4, Burroughs Park, Houston

| Circumference: 105" | Height: 70' | Spread: 96' | INDEX: 199 |

Ginkgo *(Ginkgo biloba)*
Harris County Precinct 4, Burroughs Park, Houston

| Circumference: 17" | Height: 32' | Spread: 96' | INDEX: 54 |

American Elm

{ 6 — — 7 }

THE HARRIS COUNTY
Tree Registry
SECOND EDITION

CHAMPION TREES

Hackberry *(Celtis occidentalis)*
Col & J.G. Hamblet, 10934 Bexere Loop Road, Houston

| Circumference: 185" | Height: 75 | Spread: 66' | INDEX: 276 |

Haw, Texas *(Crataegus texana)*
City of Houston, Arboretum & Nature Center

| Circumference: 20" | Height: 33 | Spread: 20' | INDEX: 50 |

Hercules Club *(Zanthoxylum clava-herculis fruticosum)*
Harris County Precinct 4, Jesse H. Jones Park, Houston

| Circumference: 36" | Height: 54 | Spread: 35' | INDEX: 79 |

Hickory, Shagbark *(Carya ovata)*
City of Houston, Arboretum & Nature Center

| Circumference: 17" | Height: 22 | Spread: 11' | INDEX: 36 |

Hornbeam, American *(Carpinus caroliniana)*
Harris County Precinct 4, Jesse H. Jones Park, Houston

| Circumference: 38" | Height: 26 | Spread: 20' | INDEX: 50 |

Jerusalem Thorn *(Parkinsonia aculeata)*
City of Houston, Fire Station 16, 1700 Richmond Avenue

| Circumference: 46" | Height: 38 | Spread: 35 | INDEX: 43 |

Laurelcherry, Carolina *(Prunus caroliniana)*
Texas Parks & Wildlife Department, Lake Houston State Park

| Circumference: 122" | Height: 35 | Spread: 40' | INDEX: 169 |

Loquat *(Eriobotrya japonica)*
Suzanne Valasek, 14003 St. Mary's Lane, Houston

| Circumference: 30" | Height: 11 | Spread: 18' | INDEX: 48 |

Hornbeam

{ 8 — — 9 }

Design Firm:
Savage Design Group,
Inc., Houston, Texas
Art Director/Designer:
Kevin Bailey
Photographer:
Jeff Heger

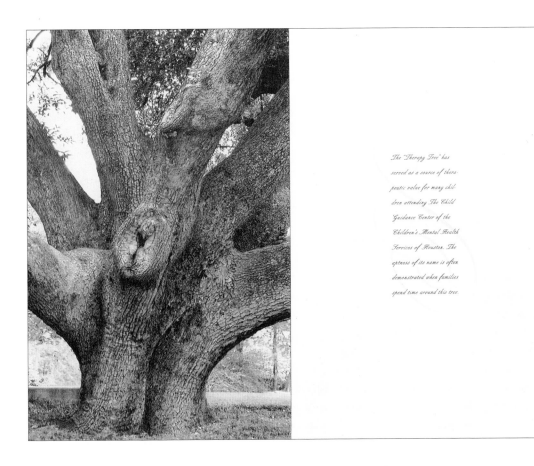

The "Therapy Tree" has served as a source of therapeutic value for many children attending The Child Guidance Center of the Children's Mental Health Services of Houston. The aptness of its name is often demonstrated when families spend time around this tree.

The Harris Country Tree Registry serves to identify and celebrate the largest and most distinguished trees in the Houston area, to increase the likelihood that the trees will be preserved. The main problem facing the Savage Design Group in creating the booklet was to make it not just inviting but saleable, to generate revenue for the organization behind the preservation effort, The Park People. Savage broke up the listing of trees with images and anecdotal copy about specific examples, such as the "Therapy Tree" and the "Old Hanging Oak." Original photographs by Jeff Heger were enhanced in Photoshop to exaggerate colors in compensation for the uncoated Simpson Coronado SST stock printed using fluorescent process mixed 50/50 with standard process. A number of black-and-white shots were modified for an antique color look. The warm, textured stock, fly sheets of handmade paper speckled with leaves, elegant type, and small format (6" x 9") combine to give the piece an intimate feel.

A woodland in full color is awesome as a forest fire, in magnitude at least; but a single tree is like a dancing tongue of flame to warm the heart.

—Hal Borland

The three booklets featuring hotels and inns displayed here share a fine-art appeal. Kolodny & Rentschler's brochure for the Charlotte Inn welcomes potential guests with evocative watercolors by Marilyn Caldwell (this spread). The images capture the unique charm of this antique-filled establishment on Martha's Vineyard, in Massachusetts. A brochure by Wood Design commemorates the installation of Raymond Mason's sculpture, "The Departure of Fruit and Vegetables from the Heart of Paris, 28 February 1969," at the Four Seasons Hotel, Washington, D.C. (p. 168). The booklet takes the form of an artist's sketchbook, tracing the development of the piece from pencil sketches through a reverse gatefold depicting the finished work. Mike McConnell traded 250 copies of a tiny booklet illustrated with his sketches of the Jamaica Inn for expenses and a free stay at the Ocho Rios resort. Though the piece could be considered to be a limited-edition artist's book, McConnell doesn't take himself too seriously: One spread examines the relative merits of sunscreens (p. 169).

Design Firm:
Kolodny & Rentschler,
Vineyard Haven,
Massachusetts
**Art Directors/
Designers:**
Mary Rentschler,
Carol Kolodny
Illustrator:
Marilyn Caldwell
Copywriter:
Mark Jenkins

A pathway leads visitors through the rose garden to the Coach House, in which is garaged a wood-paneled 1939 Ford station wagon and 1920s pony cart. Upstairs is one of the inn's most popular rooms, the Coach House Suite, which offers glimpses of Edgartown Harbor through a wonderful palladian window. During July and August, a balmy breeze cools the inn's open spaces. The Summer House's airy veranda is a first stop for guests thankful to have escaped the bustle of city life; here the only sounds may be the creak of a rocking chair, the rustle of newspaper, the clink of cubes in a glass of iced tea. By contrast, fall or winter is the time to sit by the fire and curl up in an overstuffed chair with a long-neglected book.

The inn's gardens provide a unifying counterpoint to the diverse architectural elements. From every window guests can enjoy the marriage of nature's benevolence and the dedication of the inn's team of gardeners. Immaculate lawns are punctuated by arches, tile borders, and fountains. Potted plants, English ivy, and manicured hedges underscore the distinguished air of the inn's lush gardens. The passion for nature's beauty is most fully expressed at the Garden House, where the inspiration for the plantings derives from the traditional English perennial garden.

"Edgartown's Charlotte Inn - A classic example of the traditional New England Country Inn, combining elegance with a quiet, comfortable atmosphere."
- THE BOSTON HERALD

"'Was this indeed,' I asked myself, 'the ultimate country inn bedroom?'"
- Norman Simpson COUNTRY INNS AND BACK ROADS

Exquisite craftsmanship greets the guest at every turn - a hand-founded brass door latch, meticulously refurbished bathroom fixtures, traditional French and English tiles, and antique windows and doors that have been lovingly restored to their original grandeur.

The respect for material treasures extends to the care and comfort of inn guests. Superior service is de rigeur - unobtrusive yet attentive, discreet but personalized. Individual guest preferences are accommodated with pleasure.

The Charlotte Inn turned to Kolodny & Rentschler for this brochure showcasing the high quality accommodations and services offered by the Martha's Vineyard establishment. Marilyn Caldwell, a friend of the inn's owners and an occasional guest, painted the warmly detailed watercolors over a period of five years, and her works are featured in a gallery at the inn. The images provide a preview of the guest experience, which the owners hope will evoke "a sense of having stepped back in time." Kolodny & Rentschler incorporated specific copy explaining the attractions of the antique-filled inn along with review quotes from well-known newspapers and magazines. The generous 10"-square format adds to the fine-art appeal of the piece.

THE CHARLOTTE INN

RAYMOND MASON

Wood Design created this brochure commemorating a sculptural installation by Raymond Mason as a keepsake for guests of the Four Seasons Hotel in Washington, D.C. The 6 1/2" x 7 1/2" brochure displays the creative genesis of "The Departure of Fruit and Vegetables from the Heart of Paris, 28 Feburary 1969." The development of the sculpture, which takes as its subject the final day of the picturesque Les Halles market, is followed from pencil, ink, and watercolor sketches to a reverse gatefold image of the completed work inserted at the center of the booklet. The textured cover, in Champion Hopsack, is printed with a fabric pattern and the artist's initials in the lower right-hand corner to suggest a sketchbook. Postcards isolating specific images, printed on various stocks in differing sizes, were tucked into the brochure for the convenience of hotel guests .

Design Firm:
Wood Design,
New York, New York
Art Director:
Tom Wood
Designers:
Tom Wood,
Alyssa Weinstein
Illustrator:
Raymond Mason

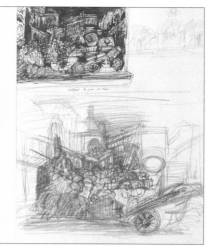

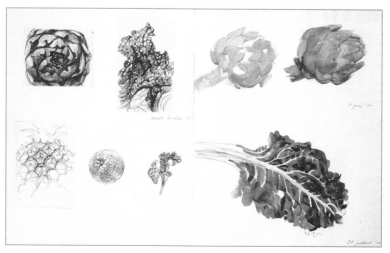

Design Firm:
Wet, Inc.,
Phoenix, Maryland
Illustrator:
Mike McConnell

JAMAICA INN

Mike McConnell reports that this tiny 5 ¼" x 7" booklet was created "to promote the uniqueness of the Jamaica Inn and the eclectic drawings of an always-for-hire artist (me)." McConnell produced the booklet in exchange for expenses and a free stay at the Ocho Rios establishment, which he visited with his wife, a travel agent. He sketched the ink drawings into a hardbound 11" x 14" book: In other words, he says, "All work done on my laptop." While McConnell can produce 15 booklets in an evening, using a Canon copier, an NEC laserprinter, and Strathmore writing and cover paper, the Jamaica Inn wanted 250 copies. He did them himself, "with help from houseguests," but admits that he'll use a printshop for similar projects in the future.

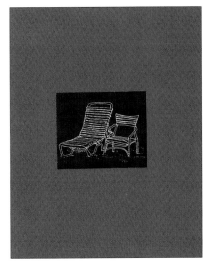